100% PHOTOSHOP

Create stunning illustrations without using any photographs

Steve Caplin

AMSTERDAM • BOSTON • HEIDELBERG • LONDON • NEW YORK • OXFORD
PARIS • SAN DIEGO • SAN FRANCISCO • SINGAPORE • SYDNEY • TOKYO

Focal Press is an imprint of Elsevier

ELSEVIER

Focal Press

Focal Press is an imprint of Elsevier
The Boulevard, Langford Lane, Kidlington, Oxford, OX5 1GB
30 Corporate Drive, Suite 400, Burlington, MA 01803, USA

First published 2010

British Library Cataloguing in Publication Data
Caplin, Steve.
  100% Photoshop : creating stunning illustrations without
  using any photographs.
  1. Adobe Photoshop. 2. Digital art.
  I. Title II. Hundred per cent Photoshop III. One hundred
  per cent Photoshop
  006.6'86-dc22

Library of Congress Control Number: 2010921650

ISBN: 978-0-240-81425-4

For information on all Focal Press publications visit our website at www.focalpress.com

Printed and bound in the United States

10 11 12 11 10 9 8 7 6 5 4 3 2 1

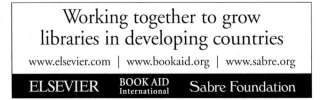

Essential techniques

Get up to speed on the basic Photoshop selection, adjustment and shading techniques.

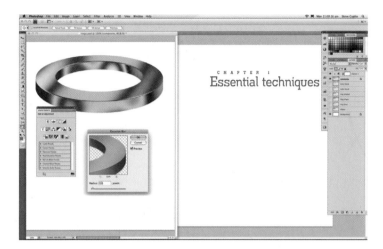

Setting the scene

Working with wood: using our wood texture to create a door, skirting board and dado rail. Plus creating torn wallpaper, painting light and shade, and distorting a view through frosted glass.

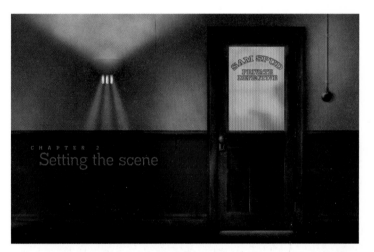

Deep Space

From a simple and quick way to paint a field of stars to super-fast planetary construction, this chapter will look at building everything from suns and spaceships to entire galaxies.

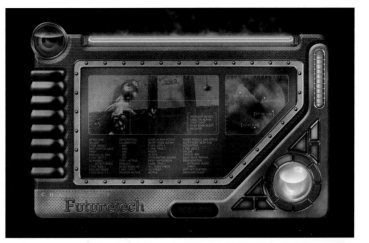

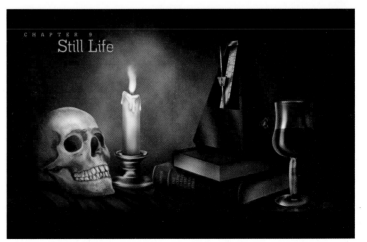

Introduction

Photoshop is the world's best-known, best-loved and just downright best photographic manipulation application. It's used by retouchers, fine artists, graphic designers, photographers, and everyone who works with images in any form.

But there's another side to Photoshop. In my work as an illustrator for newspapers and magazines, I frequently have to come up with a finished image against impossibly tight deadlines. And if I don't have a suitable photograph of a flying saucer, or a leather book from just the right angle, or an award trophy, or a paperclip, then I often end up drawing it directly inside Photoshop.

Drawing in Photoshop isn't just a second-rate alternative when we can't find the right image. When we draw an object, we can create it at exactly the shape and angle we want. We can also make it perfectly in focus, with perfect lighting. Drawn objects can be crisper and better defined than even the sharpest photograph: it can often be quicker, too, to draw something rather than to find the real thing and photograph it.

There's a real pleasure to be taken from creating an entire illustration from scratch, without using any photographs whatsoever. And while we might still use a photograph as reference material, this is no different to a conventional artist using a model or prop to draw from.

Everything in this book has been drawn entirely in Photoshop, using only the filters and tools that come with the application. Although Photoshop has got better and better with each new version, there's nothing in this book that can't be achieved with a version that's five or more years old.

Drawing from scratch in Photoshop is both hugely enjoyable and highly instructive. By creating our objects we learn a lot about how real world items reflect light, how surfaces are constructed, and how shadows can help make an image more dramatic and help it to look more realistic. And by learning to draw objects, we also improve our Photoshop skills tremendously.

This has been an enormously enjoyable book to write. I hope you get as much pleasure from using it.

Steve Caplin
London, 2010

How to use this book

Each chapter in this book begins with a double page illustration: the chapter then goes on to show how every object and texture in the illustration was created. By the end, we'll have reconstructed the opening image in every detail.

While I wouldn't expect even the most diligent reader to start at the beginning and work through every page of the book in turn, techniques are explained in full the first time they're used, and are then referred to when they appear again later. This is mainly for reasons of space, as too much repetition would simply take up too much space. I always refer readers to the page on which the full explanation appears.

The first chapter details the essential techniques that every Photoshop artist needs to master. It's quite likely you already know how to use QuickMask, or how to combine selections, or how to use the Curves dialog – in which case the explanations on the first few pages will serve as reminders. I do, however, assume you have a general working knowledge of Photoshop's tools and filters.

Keyboard shortcuts

Keyboard shortcuts are shown for both Mac and Windows platforms. They appear in the text as follows:

Mac shortcuts are shown in red: ⌘ Shift D

Windows shortcuts are shown in blue: ctrl Shift D

Shortcuts that are the same for both Mac and Windows are shown in black: Enter

Page references

Superscript numbers refer to the page in the book on which a technique is explained for the first time. So if you're instructed to use the Clouds filter [20], it means the filter is explained in full on page 20.

Got a problem?

If you get stuck, don't understand a technique or simply want to show off your work, visit the *How to Cheat in Photoshop* Reader Forum. It's a great place to ask questions – and they'll usually be answered within an hour or two. Go to this address:

www.howtocheatinphotoshop.com

...and click the button for the Reader Forum. You'll find me and other like-minded Photoshop artists ready and willing to help you out, so take the plunge and join the friendliest and most helpful online Photoshop community.

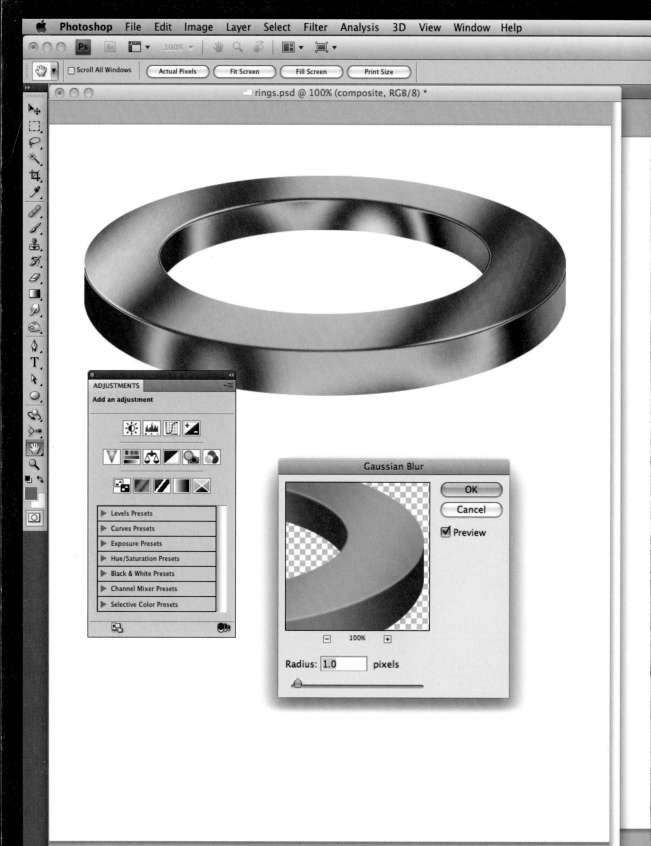

CHAPTER 1
Essential techniques

Selection tools

All Photoshop work involves making selections of one kind or another. Here's a quick primer on how to get the most out of using the tools.

The Move tool

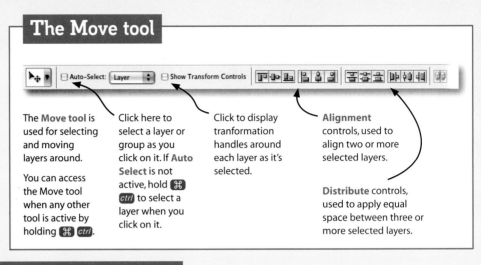

The **Move tool** is used for selecting and moving layers around.

You can access the Move tool when any other tool is active by holding ⌘ ctrl.

Click here to select a layer or group as you click on it. If **Auto Select** is not active, hold ⌘ ctrl to select a layer when you click on it.

Click to display tranformation handles around each layer as it's selected.

Alignment controls, used to align two or more selected layers.

Distribute controls, used to apply equal space between three or more selected layers.

Drawing rectangles and ellipses

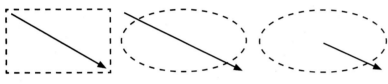

Both the **Rectangular Marquee** and the **Elliptical Marquee tools** draw from corner to corner. This can be tricky when drawing ellipses, as they have no corners; hold ⌥ alt after you start to drag to draw from the center out instead.

Hold *Shift* after you start to drag to constrain a rectangle to a square, and an ellipse to a circle.

Modifying selections

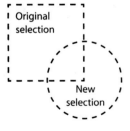

Original selection

New selection

Hold *Shift* before you make a second selection to add the new one to the old.

Hold ⌥ alt before you make a second selection to subtract the new one from the old.

Hold ⌥ Shift alt Shift to produce an intersection of the new and old selections.

Feathering selections

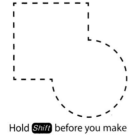

Feather Selection

Feather Radius: 6 pixels

OK

Cancel

Use **Select > Modify > Feather** to soften a selection. The original selection, filled with gray, is shown on the left; the feathered selection is shown right.

Spacebar

Hold the **Spacebar** while you're drawing a selection to move it around. When you release the Spacebar, you can continue to reshape the selection.

This makes it much easier to fit selections such as ellipses.

Painting with the brush

We'll use the Brush tool to paint a lot of the objects in this book, so the essentials are shown here.

QuickMask is a great way to make selections by painting them, rather than tracing them. But the default behavior is an awkward way of working; see below for how to change this so that selected areas are highlighted in red.

The Brush tool

Right click (*ctrl* click) with the **Brush tool** for the Brushes panel.

Click the arrow…

…to set how the thumbnails are displayed.

Drag to change the size and hardness of the current brush…

…or use **[** and **]** to make the brush smaller and larger, and **Shift [** and **Shift]** to make the brush harder and softer.

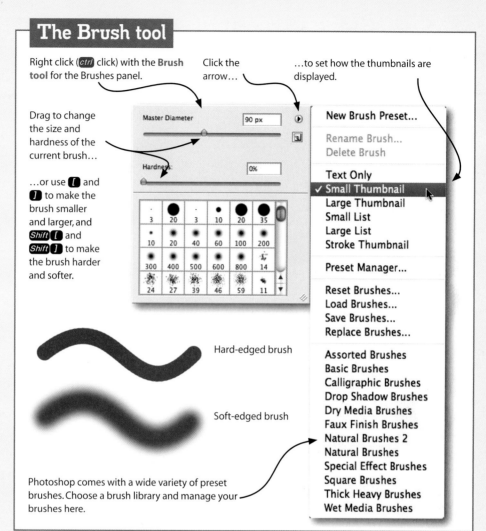

Hard-edged brush

Soft-edged brush

Photoshop comes with a wide variety of preset brushes. Choose a brush library and manage your brushes here.

QuickMask

Enter **QuickMask** by pressing **Q**. Painting in QuickMask (left) produces a corresponding selection (right) when we leave QuickMask by pressing **Q** again.

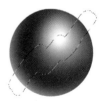

QuickMask is used to paint selections. The default behavior is to show Masked Areas, so everything *outside* the selection is highlighted.

A better way to work is with Selected Areas highlighted. To change this, double-click the QuickMask icon at the bottom of the **Tool Panel**, and click the button to change the behavior.

We can use a soft-edged **Brush**[5] to paint feathered selections. The hard and soft strokes in QuickMask (left) produce these results (right) when we leave QuickMask and delete the selection.

Working with layers

We'll create a lot of layers in the course of this book. Understanding the basics of working with layers is essential for any Photoshop artist: on these pages we'll go over techniques that everyone should know.

Locking transparency

Normally, when we paint on a layer, we can paint freely within the canvas area.

If we lock the **Transparency** of the layer, we can't paint outside the layer bounds.

To lock the Transparency, click the first icon in the **Lock** section at the top of the **Layers Panel**.
　The other icons lock the layer so it can't be painted on at all; so it can't be moved; and so it can't be modified in any way.

Free Transform

Use **Free Transform** to change a layer's size, shape or rotation. Use ⌘ T ctrl T to enter Free Transform mode, then press Enter to apply the transformation.

Drag a corner handle to scale a layer from the opposite corner; hold ⌥ alt to scale from the center.

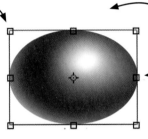

Drag *outside* the bounding box to rotate a layer.

Drag a center handle to scale in one direction.

Loading layers as selections

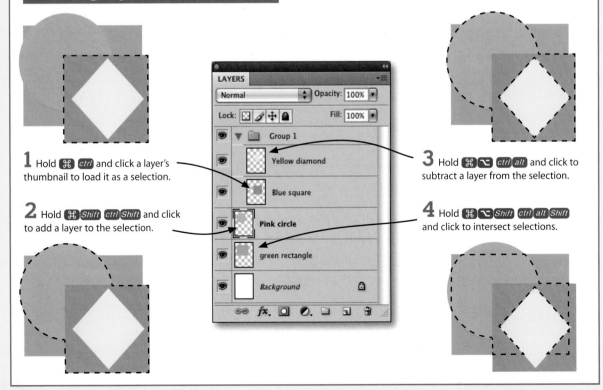

1 Hold ⌘ ctrl and click a layer's thumbnail to load it as a selection.

2 Hold ⌘ Shift ctrl Shift and click to add a layer to the selection.

3 Hold ⌘ ⌥ ctrl alt and click to subtract a layer from the selection.

4 Hold ⌘ ⌥ Shift ctrl alt Shift and click to intersect selections.

Layer Masks

Using an **Eraser tool** is an irrevocable step: once part of a layer has been erased, it's gone forever.

Using a **Layer Mask** is a better option: it's created by clicking the icon at the bottom of the **Layers Panel**, or choose **Layer > Layer Mask > Reveal All**.

Painting in black on the Layer Mask hides the layer, and painting in white reveals it again. We can paint in gray, by lowering the opacity of our brush, for partial transparency.

1 This is our original layer, a simple blue rectangle.

2 When we paint in black on the layer mask, we hide the layer.

3 This is the **Layers Panel**, showing the mask next to the layer. The black area is the active mask, which hides the layer.

We can disable a **Layer Mask** temporarily by holding *Shift* and clicking on its thumbnail.

4 If we paint with gray instead of black, we can partially hide the layer.

Adjustment Layers

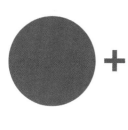

Adjustment Layers let us apply contrast, color and other adjustments to layers that are editable, and can even be turned off entirely. The advantage of Adjustment Layers is that we can apply changes that we can later adapt easily; we're also able to copy adjustments between layers. Adjustment Layers are selected from the pop-up menu at the bottom of the **Layers Panel**.

All Adjustment Layers come with a **Mask**, so we can paint out areas where we don't want the adjustment applied.

Clipping Masks

Clipping Masks are layers that constrict the visibility of the layer above. Here, the Red circle layer uses the Blue square layer as a clipping mask, so it's only visible where the two layers overlap. Multiple layers can be stacked up this way, using the bottom one as a Clipping Mask.

To make a Clipping Mask, select the uppermost layer and choose **Layer > Create Clipping Mask**. There are two alternative methods: use the shortcut ⌘ ⌥ G *ctrl* *alt* G, or hold ⌥ *alt* and click between the two layers in the **Layers Panel**.

The Curves adjustment

We'll use Curves many times to adjust a layer's brightness, contrast and color. It's a complex dialog, so here's a quick tour of its main features. Like all Adjustments, Curves can be applied directly or as an Adjustment Layer (see page 7).

The original object

1 This is the original object that we'll be applying **Curves** to.

Open the **Curves** dialog using **Image > Adjustments > Curves,** or use the keyboard shortcut ⌘ M ctrl M.

The dialog shown here is the **Curves Adjustment Layer** (see previous page), but the graph works the same in the main adjustment as well.

Basic Curves operation

2 The graph starts as a straight line. Click in the middle of the line to make a new **anchor point**, and drag upwards to brighten the midtones of the layer.

3 Drag down to darken the midtones. The Curves adjustment can be quite dramatic: usually, only a small drag is needed to create the desired effect.

4 To increase contrast, first click in the center of the graph to 'pin' the mid point, then drag up on a higher point in the curve.

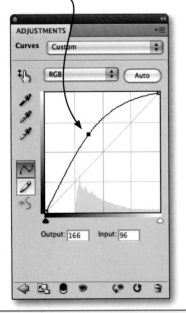

Output: 166   Input: 96

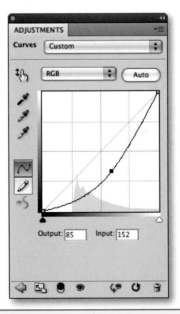

Output: 85   Input: 152

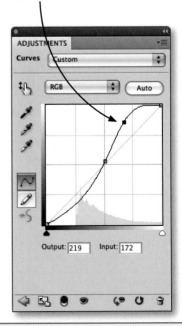

Output: 219   Input: 172

Further adjustments

5 Dragging the top right **anchor point** down reduces the brightness. Because this is an **Adjustment Layer**[7], it affects the whole artwork beneath the current layer.

6 We can make an **Adjustment Layer** operate just on the underlying layer by clicking the **Clipping Mask** icon. Now the background is not affected.

7 We can adjust the color using Curves, as well. Choosing the **Red Channel** allows us to brighten the red content of the layer, so adding a red tint to it.

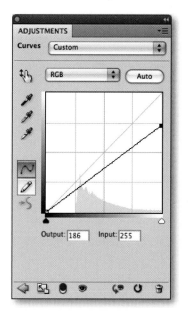

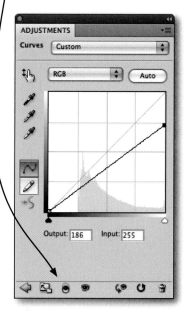

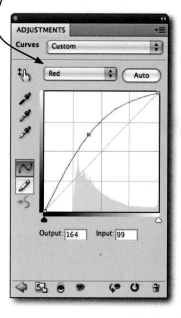

8 Adding red is one way to add color. But it tends to be rather washed out with this method. An alternative approach is to add red by reducing the amount of **Green** and **Blue**. We can do this by dragging down on the curve for both these Channels.

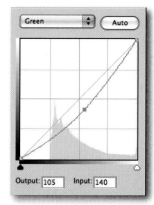

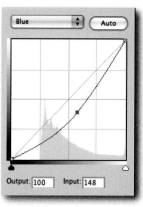

More image adjustments

Although we can perform a wide range of adjustments with just Curves (see previous pages), there are other adjustment methods that can be quicker and easier to use for a simple effect.

The original object

1 This is the original object to which we'll be applying all the adjustments on these pages.

All the adjustments can be accessed using **Image > Adjustment** and then the name of the specific adjustment. The dialogs shown here are their **Adjustment Layer**[7] equivalents, because the dialogs are neater and take up less space on the page.

Contrast

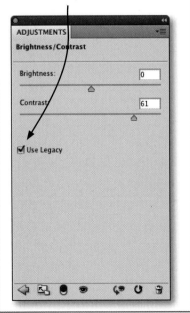

2 The **Brightness/Contrast** adjustment is a quick way to fix the contrast of a layer. Check the **Use Legacy** button for a less restrained version of the effect.

Color Balance

3 Use **Color Balance** to add color to a grayscale layer, or to adjust a layer's color. Drag the sliders to the right or left to move the hue towards the color indicated.

4 We can vary the color considerably by adjusting two or more sliders. Here, we create a simple matte gold effect.

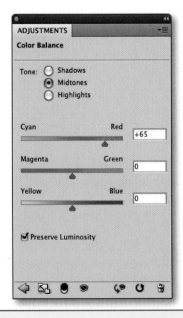

Hue/Saturation

5 The **Hue/Saturation** adjustment adjusts an object's overall color. Check the **Colorize** box to add color to a grayscale object or layer.

6 Dragging the **Hue** slider lets us adjust the overall color of the object. Moving it left and right moves us through the visible spectrum.

7 Dragging the **Saturation** slider allows us to adjust the strength of the color. Normally, we'll want to use a low saturation setting for a more realistic appearance.

Layer modes

1 We can change a layer's **Mode** to alter the way we see through it to the layers beneath. Use the pop-up menu at the top of the **Layers Panel** to change the mode. The default is **Normal**, shown here. We'll look at the main three of the other layer modes here, but check out the rest for yourself.

2 In **Multiply** mode, the sphere darkens the layer beneath; the result is a darker than either layer.

3 **Screen** mode is the opposite of **Multiply**, producing a result brighter than either layer.

4 **Hard Light** is a mode which retains highlights and shadows, while hiding the mid tones.

Basic shading

We'll use the Dodge and Burn tools a lot in this book. Here's a quick tutorial on how to use the tools to make a shaded, three dimensional ball.

We'll also look at how to make a simple shadow for the ball, using Layer Masks and the Gradient tool.

Drawing the basic shape

1 Use **Layer > New > New Layer**, then drag with the **Elliptical Marquee tool**. Hold **Shift** to draw a perfect circle.

2 Select a mid gray as the foreground color, and press ⌥ *Backspace* *alt* *Backspace* to fill the circle with gray.

Shading the ball

3 Switch to the **Burn tool**. Choose a soft edged brush, at a size about half the radius of the gray circle, and set the **Range** to **Midtones**.

4 If you're not using a pressure sensitive tablet, then set the **Exposure** to around 50% and drag around the left and bottom to add the first shading to the ball.

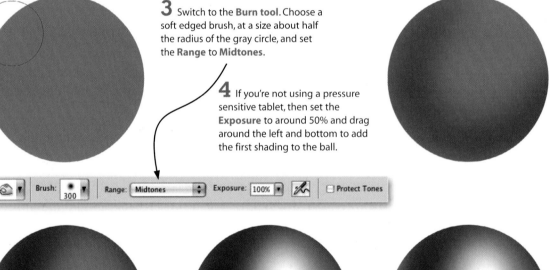

Brush: 300 | Range: Midtones | Exposure: 100% | Protect Tones

5 Continue to shade around the bottom and left of the ball until you build up a strong, deep shadow in this area.

6 Switch to the **Dodge tool**, and paint in a highlight on the ball. A handy shortcut is to hold ⌥ *alt* while using the **Burn tool**: this gives access to the **Dodge tool** temporarily.

7 Drag the **Dodge tool** around the bottom of the ball to lighten this area. This gives the impression of the ball being lit by reflected light from the surface on which it's sitting.

Creating the shadow

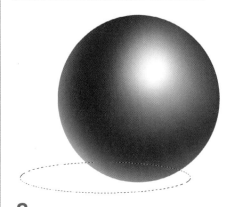

8 Make another new layer, behind the ball layer. Use the **Elliptical Marquee tool**[4] to trace a flattened ellipse, positioned so that the bottom of the ball sits about half way up the ellipse. If you hold the spacebar while drawing the ellipse, you can move it around as you draw it.

9 To soften the edge, use **Select > Modify > Feather**[4] and set a feather radius of around 20 pixels (although the exact figure will depend on how big you drew the initial ball).

10 Set the foreground color to black, and use ⌥ Backspace / alt Backspace to fill the ellipse with black.

11 Lower the opacity of the shadow layer by dragging the slider in the **Layers Panel**[6]. Choose an opacity of around 50%.

12 Make a **Layer Mask**[7] for the shadow layer by choosing **Layer > Layer Mask > Reveal All**. Switch to the **Gradient tool**, and set the tool to **Foreground to Transparent**, with the foreground color set to black.

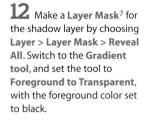

13 Drag with the **Gradient tool** from left to right across the shadow, and the **Layer Mask** will hide it progressively towards the left, producing a soft effect.

Drawing in perspective

In this tutorial we'll see how to draw a ring in perspective. Along the way we'll also use QuickMask to modify our selection, and show how to select just a thin edge to add a realistic bevel effect.

Although perspective drawing is often seen as a tricky process, this is a simple solution to the problem.

Creating the ring

1 Make a new layer, draw an ellipse with the **Elliptical Marquee tool**[4], and fill the selection with gray.

2 Without deselecting, press **Q** to enter **QuickMask**[5] mode. This will show the selected area highlighted, as shown.

3 Press ⌘ T ctrl T to enter **Free Transform**[6] mode: handles will appear around the **QuickMask** selection so it can be scaled.

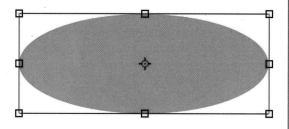

4 Hold ⌥ alt to scale it towards the center, and move the selection up so that it's nearer the top than the bottom.

5 Press **Q** again to leave QuickMask, and the red ellipse will turn into a selection. All you have to do now is to delete the selection to make the ellipse ino a perspective ring.

Perspective and shading

6 Use ⌘A ctrl A to **Select All**, then hold ⌥ alt as you nudge up a few times with the up arrow key on your keyboard. Each time you press the key, the ring will move up one pixel. Use ⌘J ctrl J to make the selection into a new layer.

7 Hide the new layer, then return to the extruded ring layer. Use the **Dodge and Burn tools** to add some vertical highlights and shadows to the ring.

8 Reveal the top ring layer once more. This is the upper surface of the ring. As it stands, the perspective doesn't quite work: the front edge is the same thickness as the back edge.

9 Enter **Free Transform** with ⌘T ctrl T, and drag the bottom center handle to make the top ring slightly shallower. This creates a thicker front edge, producing the perspective effect.

10 Use the **Dodge and Burn tools** again to add a little shading to the top surface, which stops it looking so uniformly gray.

11 Now for the bevelled edge. Hold ⌘ ctrl and click on the thumbnail of the top edge in the **Layers Panel**. With a **Selection tool** active, nudge the selection up by two pixels.

12 Inverse the selection using ⌘Shift I ctrl Shift I. Use the **Dodge tool** to brighten up the front edge, producing the bevelled effect that makes it look more like a real object.

13 Use the **Dodge tool** on the back, inside edge as well, in the same way. Congratulations! We now have a convincingly three dimensional ring.

Making metal, part 1

On the previous page we drew a ring in perspective. Despite the shading we added, it still looked like plastic.

Here we'll see a simple method to make that plastic look like gleaming metal — and then go on to turn it into gold.

The Curves graph used here is just a suggestion, though. Experiment with different Curve shapes for different results!

The Curves Adjustment Layer

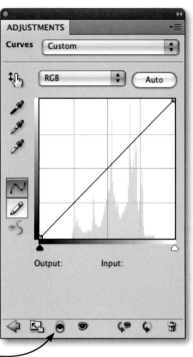

1 Start by making a new **Curves Adjustment Layer**[7]. This is chosen from the pop-up menu at the bottom of the **Layers Panel**, or, if you have Photoshop CS4 or later, from the **Adjustment Panel**.

2 To prevent the Adjustment from affecting any other layers you may have in your artwork, use the ring layer as a **Clipping Mask**. In Photoshop CS4 and later, we can do this by clicking the icon at the bottom of the panel. For earlier versions, hold ⌥ *alt* and click between the Adjustment Layer and the ring layer in the Layers Panel.

Starting the metal effect

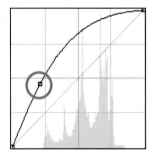

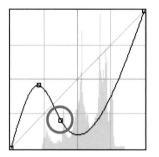

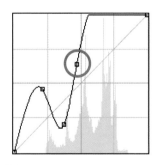

3 Click about a quarter of the way along the Curves[8] graph, and drag up a short way. This brightens the whole ring, as seen below.

4 Click around a third of the way along the graph and drag down. This will have the effect of darkening the whole ring.

5 Click a bit further along, and drag upwards once more. The ring is brightened, but we can start to see some metallic shine here.

Finishing the metal effect

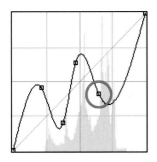 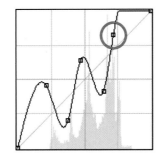 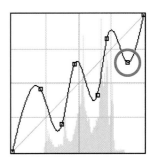

6 Click a little further along, and drag downwards. The shine is now starting to take shape, but the whole ring is still too dark.

7 Click a little further along the graph and drag up. We now have a shiny ring – but the highlights are too bright and blown out.

8 Click in the center of the remaining portion of the graph and drag down. This completes the metallic effect.

Smoothing the edges

9 The problem with the **Curves** process is that it can produce hard results at the edges. We can fix this by first locking the **Transparency**[6] of the ring layer. Click the first icon in the **Layers Panel** to do this.

10 Use **Filter > Blur > Gaussian Blur** to blur the ring about 1 pixel. We locked the transparency, so the outer edges don't get fuzzy – but the inner edges are smoothed.

Turning silver to gold

11 We can use **Color Balance**[10] to add basic color to our shiny ring. The best way to do this is with a **Color Balance Adjustment Layer**[7], placed *above* the Curves Adjustment Layer.

Alternatively, you could apply Color Balance directly to the ring layer. But if you do this, the Curves adjustment will make the colors go haywire: the solution here is to set the mode of the Curves Adjustment Layer to **Luminosity**.

Making metal, part 2

We've looked at turning plastic objects into metal. Here's an even easier way of creating a metallic effect from flat artwork – and no shading is needed to make this work. It's a Layer Style that can be applied directly to any artwork.

Use any artwork

1 Any flat artwork can be used to create this effect. I've made this simple logo, but you could draw any shape you like.

Because the effect is an **Adjustment Layer**[7], it even works on live text – which means you can edit the wording and the font after the effect has been applied.

The effect works best with smooth-cornered shapes, though. Hard corners can tend to look a little artificial.

The first bevel

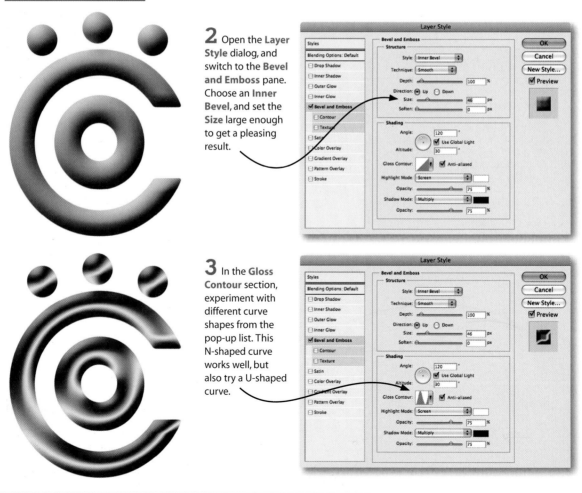

2 Open the **Layer Style** dialog, and switch to the **Bevel and Emboss** pane. Choose an **Inner Bevel**, and set the **Size** large enough to get a pleasing result.

3 In the **Gloss Contour** section, experiment with different curve shapes from the pop-up list. This N-shaped curve works well, but also try a U-shaped curve.

Adding the contour

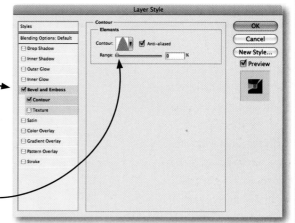

4 We can add interest and shape by adding a **Contour** to the bevel effect.

5 The **Range** slider sets the width of the effect: with the Range set to zero, we get a hard mid line.

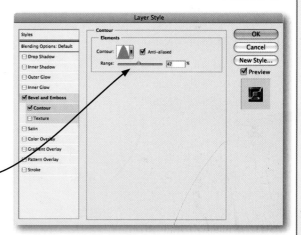

6 By varying the **Range**, we can change the appearance. Here it is set around half way along.

Experiment with different contours to see the different results produced.

7 We can add a gold effect using the **Color Overlay** section of the **Layer Style** dialog. Choose a pale brown for a gold effect. The great thing about this Layer Style is that we can paint on the layer and the effect will be applied as we paint.

The Clouds filter

If there's one thing the Clouds filter is really lousy at, it's drawing clouds. Which is a shame, given the name of the filter.

But the Clouds filter excels at creating a basic random texture, which can then be modified in many ways and put to a surprisingly large range of uses.

We'll use this filter throughout the book, as the basis for a wood texture, stone, loft insulation, a bowling ball, and dozens more objects and textural surfaces.

The basic Clouds effect

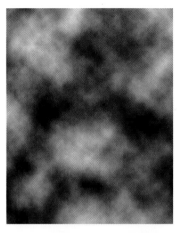

1 Start with an empty canvas, or a selection, and choose **Filter > Render > Clouds**. There's no dialog for this filter: it just performs its effect.

If you don't like the first result, you can repeat it using ⌘ F ctrl F. Each time it runs you'll get a different texture, as it randomizes the effect every time it runs.

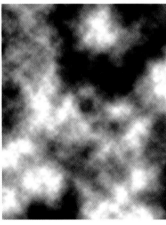

2 The only variation with the basic filter is to hold the ⌥ alt key as you choose the filter from the menu. This produces a tighter, stronger version of the effect.

Clouds and color

3 We'll generally use the default background and foreground colors of black and white when using this filter. But we can choose any pair of colors for a more subtle effect.

Here, the light and dark brown shades shown below have been set as foreground and background, to produce a soft, natural Clouds effect.

Difference Clouds

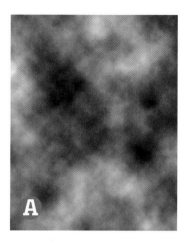

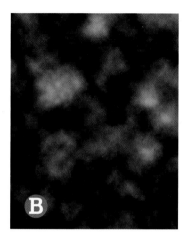

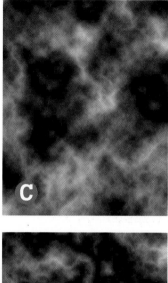

4 A variation on the standard Clouds effect is **Filter > Render > Difference Clouds**. This produces an effect that builds upon the previous result, strengthening the appearance each time.

Shown here are successive applications of the Difference Clouds filter. As we can see, each one appears to invert the texture, while making it stronger and more stylized.

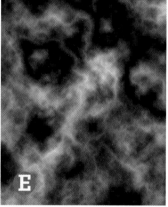

Difference Clouds with color

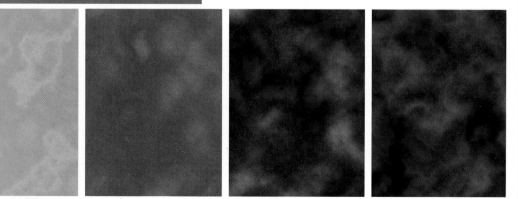

5 When we use colors other than black and white as the foreground and background shades with Difference Clouds, the colors invert each time the filter is run. Shown here are four successive applications of Difference Clouds, using purple and blue as the foreground and background colors.

The Noise filter

The Noise filter produces a random pattern of dots, at a density we can adjust.

It's useful for adding the basis of a naturalistic texture, and even a tiny amount of noise can prevent an object from looking too artificial and computer-generated.

We'll generally use Noise in conjunction with a Blur filter, to produce a soft, lumpy texture.

The basic Noise effect

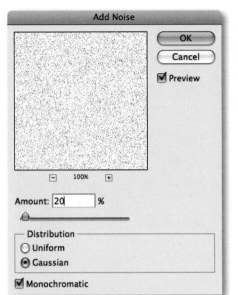

1 The Noise filter has a simple dialog – choose it from **Filter > Noise > Add Noise**. The preview shows a 100% view of the type of noise to be added, making it easy to make a selection that matches your requirements.

2 The main alternatives are **Uniform** (left) and **Gaussian** (right). Gaussian is my preferred choice, although frankly there's little to choose between them.

Color Noise

3 At the bottom of the dialog is a button marked **Monochromatic**, which produces black and white noise. If this is unchecked, we get noise full of color.

Varying the Noise effect

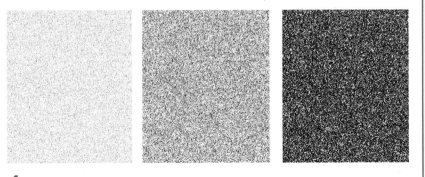

4 The **Amount** slider lets us adjust how dense the noise is. Generally, we'll want to use between 10% and 50% noise, but in special circumstances we might want less (although we'll rarely want to use more).

Shown here, from left to right, are examples of Monochromatic Gaussian Noise at values of 10%, 50% and the maximum 400%.

The Gaussian Blur filter

Blurring softens an image, and can help to stop layers looking too crisp. In this book we'll most often use this filter in conjunction with the Noise filter, as the two together can create a pleasingly random textural effect.

The basic Gaussian Blur effect

1 Choose **Filter > Blur > Gaussian Blur** to open the filter dialog. There's only one control, a slider that varies the strength of the blur by increasing its radius.

We can set the radius in 0.1 pixel increments, and we need this degree of fine control in situations such as that on page 17, when we wanted to remove the hard edges from within the drawn ring.

Gaussian Blur with Noise

2 This is the effect of the **Gaussian Blur** filter used on top of the **Noise** filter we applied on the previous page. Shown here are examples of the blur set to a radius of 1, 2, 5 and 10 pixels. There are other Blur filter types, though – some are shown below.

Other types of blur

 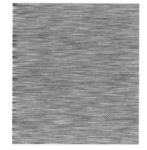 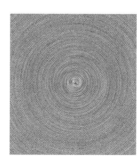 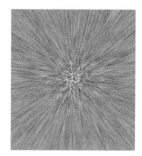

3 This is **Box Blur**, which creates a square-shaped blurring effect that can simulate depth of field.

4 **Motion Blur** simulates movement – and is a good texture base. This is 30% horizontal motion blur.

5 **Radial Blur** is good for generating circular and zooming patterns. It's available in two flavors – **Spin** (left) and **Zoom** (right). In this book we'll use Spin for creating a record surface, and Zoom for making a fantasy art background.

Wood texture

We'll use wood texture a lot in this book – but that's only because wood is used a lot in everyday life.

There are many different ways to create convincing wood. This is one of my favorites – it's relatively easy to make, and the result is a strongly grained wood that can be tinted and contrasted to suit a wide variety of purposes.

The base texture

1 Start with a plain brown layer. I'm showing a close-up of the layer here, so we can see the texture; work at any size you like.

2 Add some noise using **Filter > Noise > Gaussian Noise**[22]. Add enough **Monochromatic Noise** for a strong effect.

3 With the same brown as the foreground color, and white as the background color, run **Filter > Render > Clouds**[18]. Use **Edit > Fade Clouds** and reduce the opacity to 25%.

4 For a more natural texture, use **Filter > Blur > Motion Blur**[23] and apply a vertical blur of around 12 pixels. This creates the base upon which we'll work.

Adding the grain effect

5 Use **Filter > Distort > Wave** to make the wood grain. The settings I used are shown below. Experiment with the Wavelength settings and Randomize button, and keep trying it out until you get a decent grain effect.

Wave

Number of Generators: 514

	Min.	Max.
Wavelength:	10	402
Amplitude:	5	181

	Horiz.	Vert.
Scale:	1 %	28 %

Type:
- ● Sine
- ○ Triangle
- ○ Square

[OK]
[Cancel]

(Randomize)

Undefined Areas:
- ● Wrap Around
- ○ Repeat Edge Pixels

You may find it takes a few tries at this filter to get good results; you should end up with something like this.

Knots and whorls

Forward Warp: smudges the texture as you drag

Twirl: twists the texture clockwise or anticlockwise

Bloat: enlarges the area you paint, good for creating knots

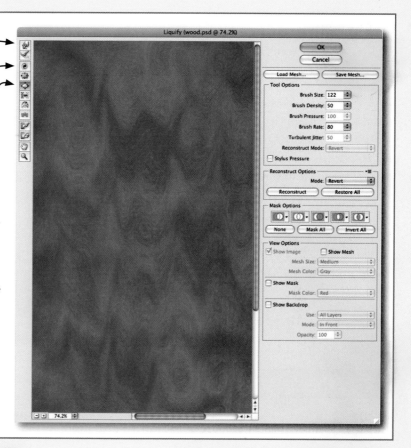

6 We could just stop at the end of the previous step – it's a fairly convincing pine-like texture. But let's take it a step further, and make something closer to mahogany, with a finer, more twisted grain.

Use **Filter > Liquify** to open this window. There are several tools we can use to distort the image: I'd recommend using **Forward Warp**, **Twirl** and **Bloat**, as shown above.

Drag within the image area, using a fairly large brush, and you should find it possible to create a convincing-looking wood texture with just a little effort. If it all goes wrong, simply **Cancel** and start the process again.

Strengthen the texture

7 The texture we've created so far may look a little washed-out – so let's beef it up. Duplicate the texture layer, and desaturate using ⌘ Shift U ctrl Shift U.

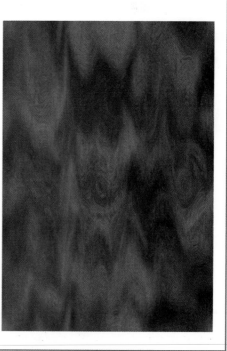

8 Change the mode of the desaturated layer from Normal to **Hard Light**[11], which allows us to see through it. Lower the layer's opacity until the effect doesn't look too strong. Here, I've also stretched the new texture vertically by about 10%, which makes for a more natural appearance.

Brick texture

The key to making effective bricks is not to make the colors too regular. This means having a simple way to select individual bricks so we can adjust them. We can't easily do this after the bricks have all been textured – but if we keep a copy of the black and white originals, it's easy to make a Magic Wand selection from that, which we can apply to our textured bricks.

Basic bricks

1 Start by drawing a single brick as a black rectangle. Although we generally work on new layers, it's best to draw this directly on the Background layer in order for the textures to work correctly.

2 Drag copies of the brick to make an array. Hold ⌥ alt as you drag to move a copy, and hold Shift to move the copy in a straight, horizontal line.

You should only need to make two rows of bricks: those can then be copied to make all the rest.

I'm showing just a section of the image here. You should work on a larger area, with a lot more bricks.

Roughening the bricks

3 Use **Filter > Distort > Glass** to roughen the edges of the bricks. The precise amount of roughening depends on the size of the bricks you're drawing, and the degree to which you want them to be distressed.

After applying this filter, duplicate the layer – you'll need to refer to this one in its current state later. It's a clean version of the artwork that makes for easier **Magic Wand** selection.

After you apply the Glass filter the bricks will have rough edges. Use **Filter > Blur > Gaussian Blur** to soften the result by about a 1 pixel radius after the Glass filter has been applied.

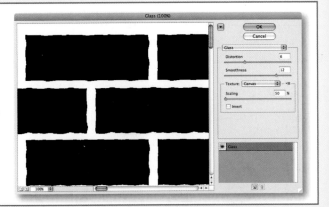

Noise and texture

4 **Filter > Render > Clouds**, then use ⌘ Shift F ctrl Shift F to fade the strength of the effect to 50%.

5 Use **Filter > Noise > Gaussian Noise** to add some roughness.

Rendering with Lighting Effects

6 With the basic texture complete, **Select All** and **Copy** the texture. Open the **Channels** panel and make a new Channel; then **Paste** the copied texture into it.

Return to the **RGB** image by clicking on **RGB** in the **Channels** panel, then make a new layer and fill with white. Choose **Filter > Render > Lighting Effects** and choose the new Texture Channel, Alpha 1, from the pop-up menu at the bottom of the dialog. Adjust the settings as shown here to render your bricks.

Color, sharpness and shadow

7 Use **Color Balance**[10] to add the basic brick color. Try settings of **50, 10, -15** for a good effect.

8 On the black and white layer created after the **Glass** filter, select the cement area with the **Magic Wand tool**. Because this layer is just black and white, it's easy to make the Magic Wand selection.
Return to the composite color layer, and use **Filter > Sharpen > Unsharp Mask** with a radius of 300 to sharpen up the cement.

9 On the black and white layer again, select some random bricks with the **Magic Wand**. Return to the color layer, and darken or lighten the selected bricks.

10 Select the cement again, then **Inverse** the selection using ⌘ Shift I / ctrl Shift I. Make a new layer above all the others, and set its mode to **Multiply**. Fill the selected area with white. You won't see anything, because white is invisible in Multiply mode. But you can use **Layer Effects** to add a **Drop Shadow** to the layer, and the shadow alone will be visible on top of the cement.

CHAPTER 2

Setting the scene

Working with wood

A significant part of this illustration is made of wood. We can use the piece of wood we created in Chapter 1, page 24 – it will work well darkened and contrasted to give a mahogany-like effect.

Shading is easily added using the Dodge and Burn tools: if we hold the Shift key as we drag with the tool, we constrain its movement to purely horizontal.

The skirting board can easily be duplicated and reused to make the dado rail – the strip of molded wood that creates a physical border between the painted wall above and the anaglypta wallpaper below.

We can also repurpose the dado rail to make the door frame, as well as the vertical and horizontal sections of the door itself.

Creating the skirting board

1 Start with a piece of wood – see page 24 for how this is created.

2 Make a selection that encloses the top section of the wood.

3 Switch to the **Burn tool**[12] (**O**). Hold *Shift* and drag horizontally to add shading at the bottom of the selection.

4 Use the **Dodge tool** to brighten the top of the selection (you can hold *⌐ alt* when using the **Burn tool** to access **Dodge** temporarily).

5 Inverse the selection using *⌘ Shift I ctrl Shift I*, and apply similar shading to the other half of the piece of wood.

Length and detail

6 Stretch the wood horizontally to make it long enough.

7 Duplicate the piece and squeeze vertically to make a narrow band.

8 Place the two pieces of wood together to make the decorative skirting board.

Building the door frame

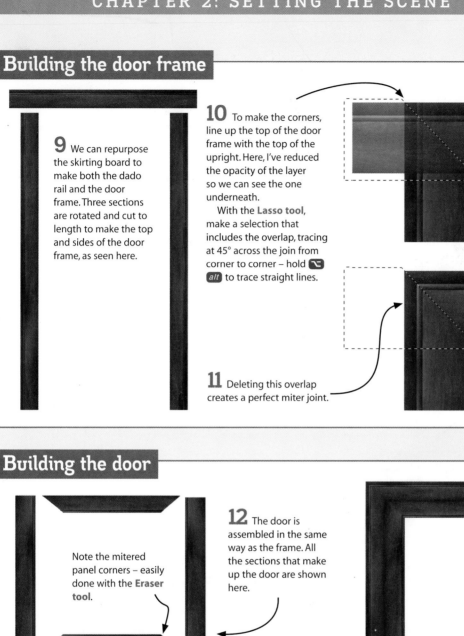

9 We can repurpose the skirting board to make both the dado rail and the door frame. Three sections are rotated and cut to length to make the top and sides of the door frame, as seen here.

10 To make the corners, line up the top of the door frame with the top of the upright. Here, I've reduced the opacity of the layer so we can see the one underneath.

With the **Lasso tool**, make a selection that includes the overlap, tracing at 45° across the join from corner to corner – hold *alt* to trace straight lines.

11 Deleting this overlap creates a perfect miter joint.

Building the door

Note the mitered panel corners – easily done with the **Eraser tool**.

12 The door is assembled in the same way as the frame. All the sections that make up the door are shown here.

13 When put together, these pieces make up the completed door.

Strangely enough, this is more or less how a real door is made – except carpenters don't have an Undo button.

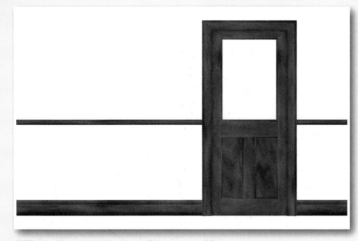

Embossed wallpaper

With the woodwork now in place, we can turn our attention to the wallpaper. This style of embossed paper is called 'anaglypta', and was popular from the 19th Century onwards.

This wallpaper is easy to create, only requiring some thought and planning when drawing the initial design.

The repeating pattern

1 Draw the initial design with a hard-edged brush on a white layer. It needs to be fairly intricate, with swirls and a suggestion of leaves and floral elements. Work within an imaginary rectangular area, and aim to more or less fill the space with your design.

2 Select the design with a rectangular marquee tool, just cutting the right hand edge short. Hold **⌥** *alt* as you drag to make a copy, and **Shift** to move it horizontally; then use **Edit > Transform > Flip Horizontal** to flip the selection.

The embossing effect

5 To create the embossed effect, use **Filter > Stylize > Emboss**. Because our design is in black on a white background, only the edges are highlighted; both the black and the white areas are turned to 50% gray by the process. This gives us a neutral ground to use as the basis for our wallpaper.

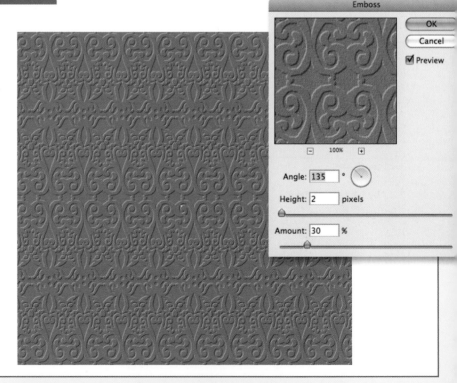

3 Select the whole design once more, clipping the edges slightly to make the joins overlap. Drag a copy out to the side, and more beneath: flip these vertically to complete the repeating pattern.

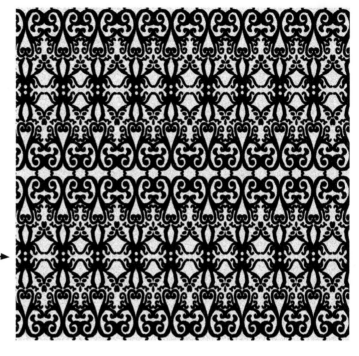

4 You can, if you like, define this area as a pattern (**Edit** menu), but it's just as easy to hold ⌥Shift alt Shift as you drag it around to make multiple copies to fill the wallpaper space.

Adding the color

6 We can use the **Hue/Saturation**[11] dialog to add color to our wallpaper. drag the hue slider first to get the right color, then the Saturation and Lightness sliders to adjust the brightness and density of the color. I've gone for a strong, deep red that's typical of the period.

Hue/Saturation

Preset: Custom

Master

Hue: 0

Saturation: 46

Lightness: -43

OK
Cancel

☑ Colorize
☑ Preview

7 Checking the **Colorize** box allows us to tint the gray surface.

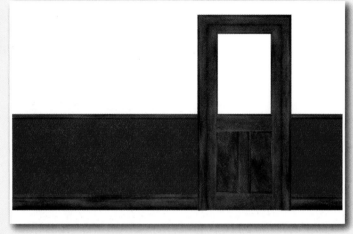

Aging the wallpaper

The wallpaper we created in the previous steps is all very well, but it's far too clean to be convincing. To age it, we need to add some dirt.

Adding splits at regular intervals gives the impression that the paper has shrunk slightly with age. We can also tear off whole sections – but we must remember to build a wall behind the tears.

Dirty stains

1 To make the wallpaper look less new, we can dirty it up. Rather than painting directly onto the layer, make a new layer and set it to **Hard Light** mode: painting on this layer in brown will have a color and darkening effect on the wallpaper, without damaging it – we can always erase any mistakes later.

The paper edge

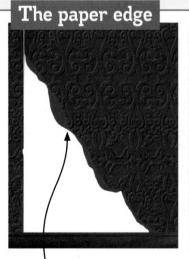

5 Make a new layer, using the wallpaper as a clipping mask (shortcut: ⌘ ⌥ G ctrl alt G). Paint a brown edge on here that only roughly follows the paper edge, to create a sense of torn paper.

6 Add a second layer, again using the wallpaper as a clipping mask, and paint with a darker shade of brown. Add a little **Gaussian Noise**[22] to add some texture.

The wall behind

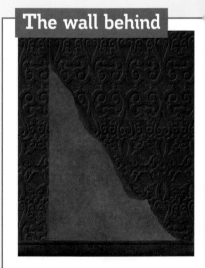

7 The wall behind is created using the **Clouds** filter for basic texture, followed by a little **Gaussian Noise**[22] and then a little **Gaussian Blur**[23]. Adjust colours for a plaster effect – we want browns and pale pinks.

Splits and tears

2 To age the wallpaper further, we need to tear some chunks out of it. Rather than deleting parts of the layer, create a **Layer Mask**[7] using **Layer > Reveal All**. Paint on the mask using a hard-edged brush, in black, to hide the layer where you paint.

4 Making a small section of the gaps a little wider helps to give the impression of the wallpaper peeling away at the edges.

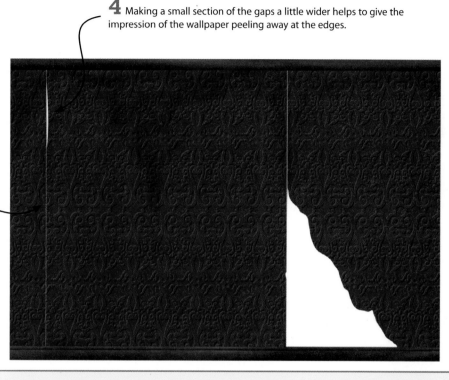

3 Make a narrow vertical selection on the layer mask with the marquee tool, and fill with black (use `⌥ Backspace` `alt Backspace`) to create vertical gaps simulating the edges of the paper roll.

8 The wooden laths are strips of the original wood texture, placed on a new layer behind the wallpaper layer.

9 Chunks of the laths can be hidden using a **Layer Mask**, to give them an old, chipped-away look. See page 7 for more on Layer Masks.

10 Adding a drop shadow using the **Layer Styles**[18] dialog gives the laths a sense of slight distance from the wall behind.

11 To make the wall look like it's truly behind the paper, make a new layer and paint a shadow on here in black, using a soft edged brush. Use a low opacity and build the shadow up slowly.

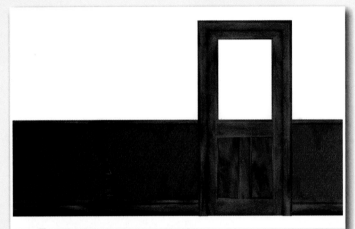

Back wall and floor

The back wall is another mottled, tobacco-stained simulation of an old paint job. Creating a few splits between the rolls of paper will add to the appearance of aging, bringing extra texture and interest to the rear top half of the image.

Wallpaper texture

1 The wallpaper texture is straightforward – the same technique we've used before. Choose two shades of brown for the foreground and background colors, and run **Filter >Render > Clouds**[18]. Add a little **Gaussian Noise**[22], then run a small amount of **Gaussian Blur**[23] to soften the result. We end up with an all-purpose stained wall effect.

Wallpaper joins

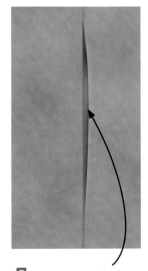

2 To make the wall look older, make thin, evenly spaced vertical selections with the **Marquee tool**. Use the **Burn tool** to add vertical stripes – but don't make the shading too regular.

3 We're going to put a split into one piece of wallpaper. Begin by drawing the shape with the **Pen tool**: curved on one side, straight up the paper join. It's shown here as a filled shape just for clarity – we're only going to work with it as a selection.

4 Use the **Burn tool** to add shading inside the split – but try to keep it to the edges, so the middle remains largely unshaded.

5 Darken the interior, then inverse the selection and use the **Dodge tool** to add a faint highlight to the right edge. This gives the paper some thickness, adding to the realism.

Creating the floor perspective

6 The floor is created using our wood texture technique (see page 24). To make the perspective effect, zoom out of the image so the gray background is visible – press **F** to hide the window edges.

Enter **Free Transform**[6] with ⌘ T ctrl T, and hold ⌘ ⌥ Shift ctrl alt Shift as you drag a bottom corner handle sideways: this creates a symmetrical perspective distortion.

Finishing the door frame

7 The floor needs to be darkened considerably to give the aged effect. Note how the bottom of the door frame is shaped to follow the shape of the molding: this is easily done with the **Eraser tool**.

Glazing the door

The glazed door will give the impression of a lit room within, which will stand out against the gloomy hall.

Drawing the interior window shape is surprisingly tricky – but it's worth going into the process in detail so we can see how these shapes are created.

The inner window shape

1 Fill a circle with color, and make a rectangular selection the same width.

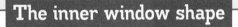

2 Fill the new selection with the same color as the circle.

3 Make a thin horizontal selection, and delete this from the window area.

4 With a **selection tool** active, drag the selection down and delete twice more.

5 Make two more vertical selections and delete in the same way.

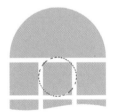

6 Draw a circle as wide as the center gaps: this is easiest drawn over the gaps themselves. See page 6 for more about drawing selections.

7 Hold ⌥ *alt* before drawing a smaller circle inside, to remove this circle from the original selection (see page 6).

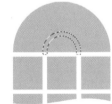

8 With a **selection tool** active, move the selection up. Remove the lower half of the selection by holding ⌥ *alt* as you drag over it with the **Marquee tool**, then delete.

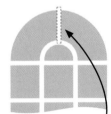

9 Make a new vertical selection and delete.

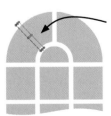

10 Use **Select > Transform Selection** to rotate, then delete the selection from both sides of the window.

Combining the elements

11 Make a new layer behind the door. Fill a selection slightly larger than the window with a flat color, then move the new window shape on top and offset it. On another layer, paint the outline of a sinister figure. It doesn't need to be accurate.

12 Merge the three layers together, and use **Filter > Blur > Gaussian Blur** [23] to soften the image by a large amount. This will help the filter used in the next step.

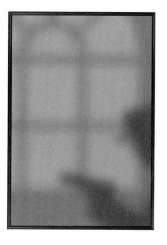

Adding the glass texture

13 Use **Filter > Distort > Glass** to add this rippling effect to the window. Experiment with the settings until you get a result that looks like convincing rippled glass.

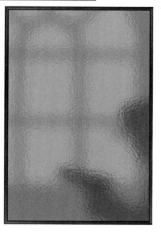

14 The window can be recolored using **Hue/Saturation** [11], or with an **Adjustment Layer** [7]. The aim is to make it look lit from within. But don't make it too bright: the rest of the hall will be in shadow.

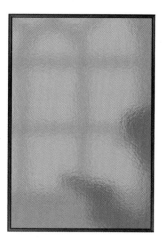

15 To make the vertical lines, first make a narrow selection and use the **Gradient tool** to apply a black to white gradient. Hold **Shift** as you drag to make the gradient purely horizontal.

16 Now duplicate the line several times.

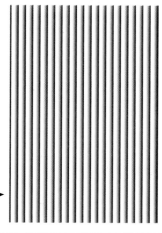

17 Change the layer mode to **Multiply** [11] so the white disappears, and lower the opacity to around 10%.

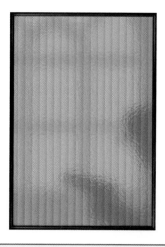

Drawing the door handle

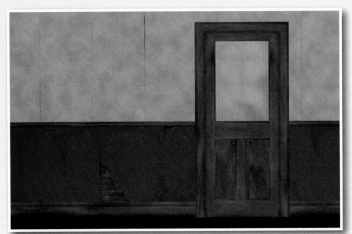

The door handle is a fiddly item to create. But it teaches us a lot about creating metallic objects, as it combines flat surfaces with curved elements, raised screws with recessed screw holes.

As with a lot of artwork creation, it's best to draw in gray and then add the color later.

The base plate

1 Begin by drawing a gray rectangle.

2 Use the **Dodge** and **Burn tools**[12] to add some basic light and shade.

3 Make a selection slightly smaller than the shape, inverse it and add shading to the outer edges.

4 Deselect the tops and bottoms, cutting the corners at a 45° angle, and add a little more shadow to crisp the corners.

5 Select the inner rectangle and add a 3pt white stroke using **Edit > Stroke**: choose an opacity of just 30% to get a faint white line that helps to mark out the edges.

The keyhole

6 Draw the keyhole on a new layer. It's a simple black circle and rectangle aligned together.

7 We can create the shading using a **Layer Style**. In the Bevel and Emboss section choose **Outer Bevel**, with a lot of depth to create the crisp highlight on the right and shadow on the left.

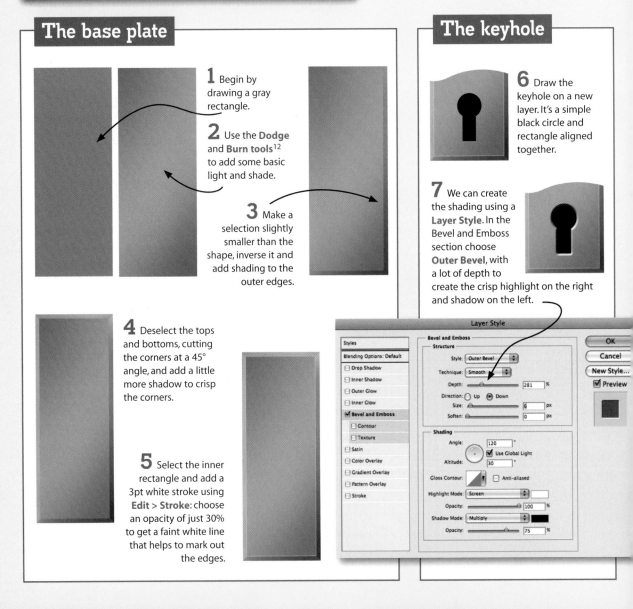

The screws

8 To make the screws, first make a gray circle on a new layer and use **Bevel and Emboss** again to add shading in the **Down** direction.

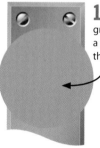

9 That was the hole; now for the screw. Make a slightly smaller gray circle and apply **Bevel and Emboss** again, this time in the **Up** direction.

10 Duplicate the screws and holes to make four of each, one in each corner of the base plate.

11 We can make the screw head slots automatically, by deleting straight lines from them: the Layer Style will create the shading for us. The easiest method is to use a small hard-edged **Eraser**, and click one side of the screw; then hold *Shift* and click the other side, and a straight line will join the two clicks.

The doorknob

12 Make a gray circle on a new layer for the knob.

13 With the **Burn tool**, add shading to the right side of the knob.

14 Use the **Dodge tool** to add a highlight at upper left.

15 Add another small highlight on the right side for a more metallic look.

The brass effect

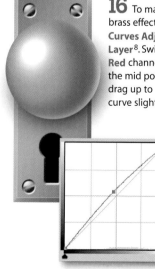

16 To make the brass effect, make a **Curves Adjustment Layer**[8]. Switch to the **Red** channel, click the mid point and drag up to raise the curve slightly.

17 Switch to the **Blue** channel, and drag the curve down to take some of the blue out of the mix. This is equivalent to adding yellow.

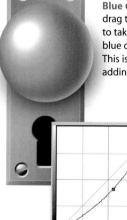

18 Switch to the **RGB** composite channel, and lower the curve to deepen the brass effect.

Finishing the door

There are only a few pieces of door furniture left to add: the hinges and the lettering. Since we've already drawn a brass door handle, we can repurpose this to make the hinges. Not only will we save time, we'll also be sure that the hinges match the tone, color and shading of the handle.

Brass hinges

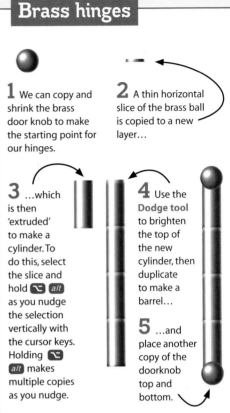

1 We can copy and shrink the brass door knob to make the starting point for our hinges.

2 A thin horizontal slice of the brass ball is copied to a new layer…

3 …which is then 'extruded' to make a cylinder. To do this, select the slice and hold ⌥ *alt* as you nudge the selection vertically with the cursor keys. Holding ⌥ *alt* makes multiple copies as you nudge.

4 Use the **Dodge tool** to brighten the top of the new cylinder, then duplicate to make a barrel…

5 …and place another copy of the doorknob top and bottom.

Beefing up the door

6 The door and wallpaper could do with some strengthening of tone, as they're starting to look a little insipid. For the door, duplicate all the layers and merge them together; then change the mode of this combined layer to **Hard Light**[11], and lower its opacity to around 50%.

For the wallpaper, create a new **Curves Adjustment Layer**[8] above the wallpaper and use this to darken the wallpaper for a better match with the new door color.

Lettering on the door

7 The font I've used here is Egyptian MT, a standard system font. It fits the 1930s period of the piece well.

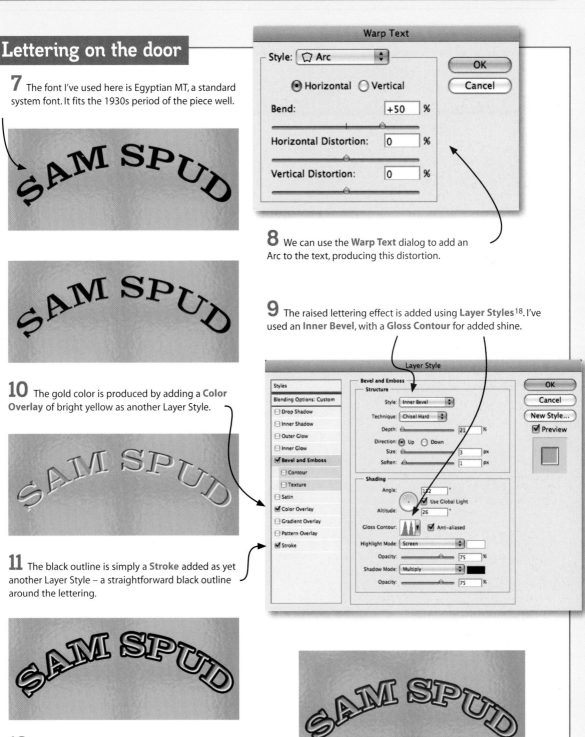

8 We can use the **Warp Text** dialog to add an Arc to the text, producing this distortion.

9 The raised lettering effect is added using **Layer Styles**[18]. I've used an **Inner Bevel**, with a **Gloss Contour** for added shine.

10 The gold color is produced by adding a **Color Overlay** of bright yellow as another Layer Style.

11 The black outline is simply a **Stroke** added as yet another Layer Style – a straightforward black outline around the lettering.

12 Straightforward lettering is used for the job title. Hold ⌥ *alt* as you drag the Layer Style from the Sam Spud layer to the new layer in the **Layers Panel**, and the style will be copied across.

To make the lettering look more part of the door, I've reduced the opacity of the layers to around 60%.

The light switch

The light switch is made of Bakelite, a dense, brittle precursor to plastic. This kind of shading is easy to create.

The cable is hidden inside metal trunking, which has been painted the same color a the walls. When we make the trunking clips, a little shading either side of the pipe will make them to look as if they're bending around it; it's a simple but effective illusion.

Drawing the light switch

1 Begin by drawing a gray circle on a new layer. Load up the circle as a selection by holding ⌘ ctrl and clicking on its thumbnail in the Layers Panel.

2 Use **Select > Modify > Contract** to shrink the selection by 3 pixels. Inverse the selection with ⌘ Shift I ctrl Shift I, and add shading to the outer rim.

3 Inverse the selection once more to get back to the inner circle, and use **Dodge and Burn** again to add a highlight top left, and shadows bottom right.

4 Adding a crescent highlight at the bottom gives the impression of a more reflective surface. Contract the circular selection, and **Dodge** the bottom edge.

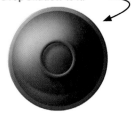

5 Draw a circular ring, and use **Layer Styles** to add an **Inner Bevel** and **Drop Shadow** to it.

6 To make the inner part of the switch, it's easiest to duplicate the switch base and scale it down using **Free Transform**. Darken it slightly so that it looks as if it's recessed within the outer ring.

7 The switch itself is drawn as a simple rectangle, fading away towards the bottom as it merges into the rocker base.

8 Make a new rectangular selection of the top of the switch, and use the **Dodge tool** to add highlights to it.

The screws are drawn in the same way as they were on the door handle – or, to save time, simply copy them from there and add to the light switch.

Adding the trunking

9 Switches of the period tended to be surface mounted. First, a short collar is added sticking out of the top of the switch assembly – this is simply a shaded rectangle with rounded corners. Then the whole switch is tinted using either **Curves**, **Levels**, or **Color Balance** (your choice) to give it a Bakelite brown feel.

10 To make the trunking, first make a new layer and fill with a color sampled from the wallpaper. Use the **Clouds** filter to add some slight texture (left).

11 Use the **Dodge and Burn tools** to add shading to the trunking – light on the left, dark on the right.

The trunking clips

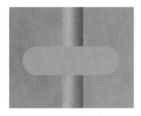

12 Make a new layer and draw a lozenge shape with the **Rounded Rectangle Shapes tool**. Fill with a color sampled from the wallpaper.

13 Use the **Dodge and Burn tools** to add a highlight to the top and left of the lozenge, and a shadow to the bottom and right. This shading should be very thin, as the clip is a thin piece of painted metal.

14 Add indentations and screwholes in the same way as we added them to the door handle – or copy them from there.

15 More shading on either side of the trunking creates the impression of the clip curving over it: use **Dodge and Burn** again.

More shading

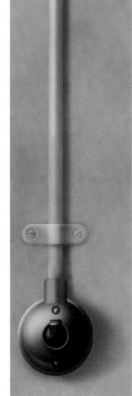

16 Darken the pipe beneath the clips to cast a slight shadow. Make a new layer behind the entire switch assembly, and paint in a shadow beneath it. At the bottom, the shadow should be elongated to the right so it appears to be cast from a distant light source.

Light and shade

With the hall furniture just about complete, it's time to add the most important element of all: the lighting.

We'll begin by creating the light source, a simple bowl-shaped uplighter with projecting glass highlights beneath. This will allow us to create attractive lighting shapes on the wall, adding a sense of drama to the scene.

The glass projections

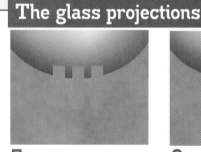

5 Start by drawing three round-cornered rectangles, cutting their tops square where they enter the lamp bowl.

6 Add random shading to the edges with the **Burn tool** – don't be too even.

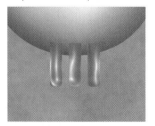

7 Use **Filters > Artistic > Plastic Wrap** to turn that shading into shiny glass.

8 Add a little green coloring to the glass, using **Curves** or **Color Balance**.

The light bowl

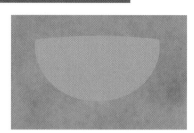

1 To draw the shape of the bowl, first make a circular selection. Then hold ⌥ ⌘ *alt* *ctrl* and draw a much larger elliptical selection over it: the result will be the intersection of the two[4]. The top of the bowl here is the top of the second selection.

2 Fill the selection with a color taken from the wall, and add shading at the edges to give it some roundness.

3 Add a highlight using the **Dodge tool**, completing the roundness of the bowl shape.

4 On a new layer behind the bowl, paint a small amount of white with a soft brush to make the lamp glow.

Building the shadow

9 There are several ways to add a lot of shadow; this is one of the most flexible.

Begin by making a new layer above all the others, and fill with dark gray – around 80% black. Make a **Layer Mask** for this layer[7].

With the **Marquee tool**, make a rectangular selection that matches the shape of the door window, and fill this with black on the Layer Mask. This will hide this area on the shadow layer, allowing us to see through it.

10 When we change the mode of the new shadow layer from **Normal** to **Hard Light**[11], we can see through even the darkest parts of the layer to the illustration beneath. By changing the opacity of this layer, we can vary the overall strength of the mask.

11 We need to paint the light coming out of the lamp. To do this, we paint in black on the Layer Mask, hiding the shadow layer; the advantage of this approach is that we can paint in white on the mask to reveal it again, adding shadow back.

Use a soft-edged brush to paint a triangular shape coming out of the top of the lamp. Use softer and larger brushes as you paint higher, to exaggerate the spread of the light further from the lamp.

Building the shadow (continued)

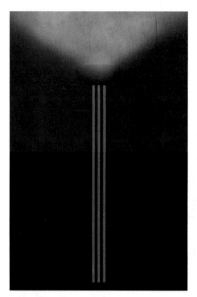

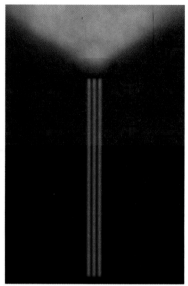

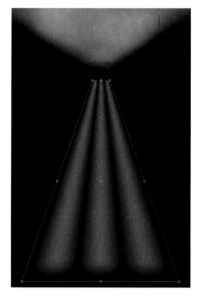

12 To paint the light coming through the glass projections beneath the lamp, first enter **QuickMask** mode[5]. Create three identical black vertical rectangles directly beneath the glass: they'll show as red rectangles in QuickMask.

13 Use **Filter > Blur > Gaussian Blur**[23] to add blur of around 6 pixels in radius. This softens the edges of the vertical bars, and will prepare them for the step that follows.

14 Enter **Free Transform** using ⌘T ctrl T, and hold ⌘ ⌥ Shift ctrl alt Shift as you drag one of the corner handles sideways to produce this perspective effect. Note how the 6 pixel blur we applied to the bars has become greatly exaggerated as we distort them.

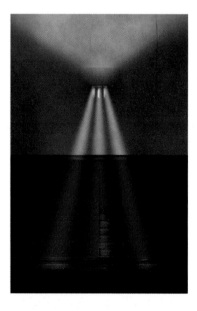

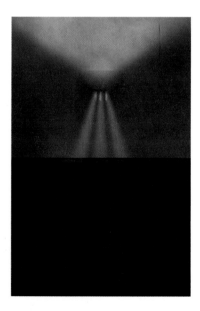

15 Press Q once more to exit QuickMask mode, and – still working on the Layer Mask attached to the shadows layer – fill the resulting selection with black. This will hide the selected area on the mask, allowing the image below to show through at full strength.

16 In fact, the result we get is just a bit too strong and well-defined. So use a large, soft-edged brush to paint the bottom of the rays in white on the mask, which will reveal the shadow layer again where we paint, so reducing the effect of the light rays and making them more convincing.

Softer edges

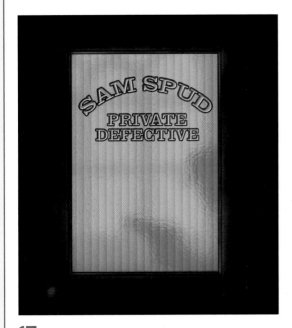

17 Paint on the shadow **Layer Mask** in black with a soft **Brush** around the edge of the window, to blur and soften the hard edge we left there.

18 Using a soft-edged brush again, paint the bottom of the door on the Layer Mask, radiating out very slightly into the hall, to give the impression of light inside the room.

Extra patches of light

19 We now need to let more light into the image generally. Using a large, soft brush, and at a low opacity, paint in black on the Layer Mask to hide the shadow around the image: around the light switch, next to the door, a little on the bottom of the door and the wallpaper. The idea here is to add the sense of light reflected from other sources, and to brighten up the image sufficiently for us to see what's going on. Add a dark shadow down the right side of the door frame, away from the lamp.

Finally, bring the three glass projections on the lamp to the top of the **Layers Panel**.

CHAPTER 3

Deep Space

Starry, starry night

It's always night time in space. It's also very cold. Which is probably why no-one chooses to live there. (That, and the fact that the atmosphere is dead.)

We could paint our stars in one at a time, but that would be a slow, painful business. Instead, we can create stars far more quickly by first defining a new Photoshop brush with which to draw them.

Creating custom brushes is a technique we'll return to again in this book, and it's worth getting the basics nailed down so that we can make full use of this interesting technology. So here's a relatively straightforward brush to start us off.

Defining the star brush

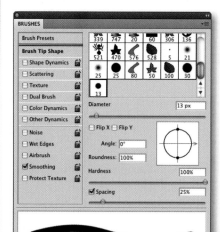

1 Begin by selecting a small, round, hard-edged **Brush**[5] – around 12 pixels or so works well, depending on the size you want your stars to end up. Open the **Brushes Panel** from the **Window** menu, and you'll be able to start customizing tbe Brush. As it stands, the Brush paints a solid line, as shown below. The first thing we need to do is to address the spacing to move the Brush tips apart.

4   The stars still trace a firm path along the line we draw when using the Brush. Switch to the **Scattering** pane, and set the **Scatter** value to 1000% (the maximum amount). Now the dots will waver either side of the Brush stroke.

5   To add some more randomness into the stars' behavior, drag the **Count Jitter** slider to 100%. This will vary the number of stars painted.

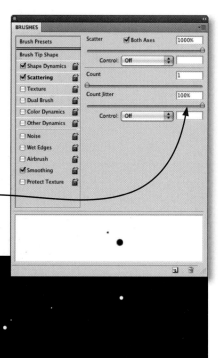

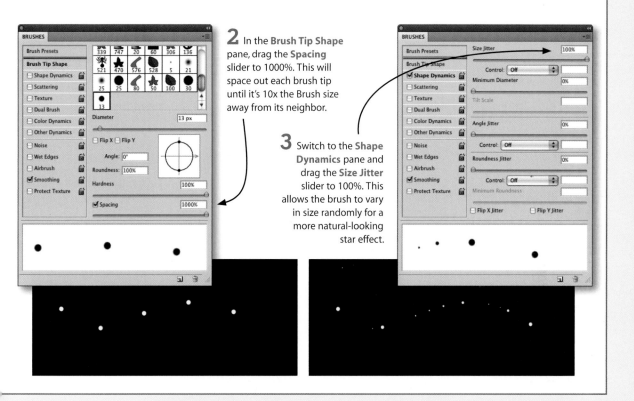

2 In the **Brush Tip Shape** pane, drag the **Spacing** slider to 1000%. This will space out each brush tip until it's 10x the Brush size away from its neighbor.

3 Switch to the **Shape Dynamics** pane and drag the **Size Jitter** slider to 100%. This allows the brush to vary in size randomly for a more natural-looking star effect.

6 Now is a good time to save that Brush. Choose **New Brush Preset...** from the pop-up menu at the top right corner of the **Brushes Panel**, and give it a name.

7 Set your background layer to black, and make a new layer above it. With white as the foreground color, start to scribble with the **Brush tool** and you'll see the black gradually filling up with stars. Here, I painted stars in just a corner of the artwork, about a quarter the size of the full image, rather than filling the entire area with stars.

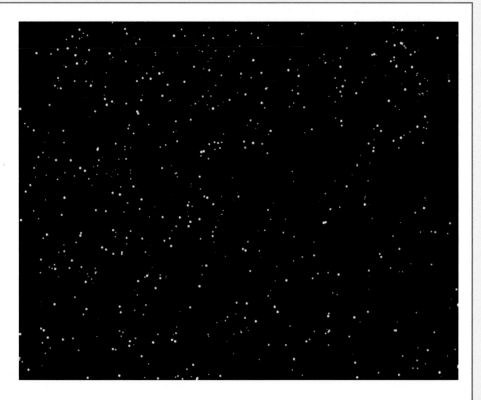

Completing the stars

1 Despite our best efforts to space the stars out, they still paint themselves too close together. So when I painted my stars I only painted a quarter of the image area, and then used **Free Transform** to blow this up to fill the entire space. This resulted in stars that were more widely spaced, but which were now too large.

2 To make the individual stars smaller, hold ⌘ *ctrl* and click on the star layer's name in the **Layer Panel** to load them as a selection[6]. Now choose **Select > Modify > Contract** and reduce the size of the selection by one or two pixels. Then inverse the selection using ⌘ *Shift* *I* *ctrl* *Shift* *I* and delete, to leave smaller stars.

3 The glow is added using the **Layer Style** dialog[17]: add an **Outer Glow**, changing its color to white.

4 Bright white looks too strong for our stars – we want to make them dimmer. But if we simply lower the opacity of the layer, the glow will dim as well. Instead, open the **Layer Style** dialog again and lower the **Fill** amount. This makes the stars dimmer without affecting the glow.

5 To complete the effect, I've created a new layer and painted a second set of stars using the original brush we created. These are much more sparse, and are smaller because we haven't enlarged this version. The result is a much more convincing star field.

Planetary construction

With the star background complete, it's time to turn our attention to the first planetary object – that Mars-like sphere hanging in space. Although the surface looks complex, it's easily created using the Clouds filter, which we'll end up using several times in this image.

Drawing the planet

1 Because Mars is a red planet, we'll start with a red blob. Make an elliptical selection on a new layer, holding **Shift** to constrain it to a perfect circle. Set the foreground color to red, and use **Backspace** *alt* **Backspace** to fill the selected area with this color. Do not deselect at this stage – we need the selection for the next steps.

Disc into sphere

4 In order to make the object look more like a planet and less like a flat disk, we need to turn it into a sphere. Using, of course **Filter > Distort > Spherize**. Go for the default (maximum) value. You'll need to make sure the outline is still selected before using this filter.

Spherize

OK
Cancel

-   100%   +

Amount   100   %

Mode   Normal

2 With the foreground color set to red and the background to black, choose **Filter > Render > Difference Clouds**[21]. The result will be a basic Cloud-like filter, as seen here.

3 The **Difference Clouds** filter doesn't behave quite the same as the regular **Clouds** filter: each time it's applied it changes the effect slightly. Use ⌘F / ctrl F to repeat the filter a few times until you get an effect you like.

Shading and glowing

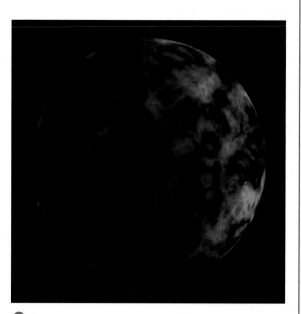

5 We want our light source (the sun) to be on the right, so we need to add some shading. Using the **Dodge** and **Burn** tools[12], paint a bright highlight on the right and shadow on the left.

6 For a more ethereal look, open the **Layer Style** dialog and add an **Outer Glow**. Change the default yellow to a red, sampled from the planet's surface.

Creating the planet earth

Now that we've got Mars under our belt, a simple spot of terraforming shouldn't present us with too much of a problem.

The planet we're going to build here is loosely earth-based in that it's essentially blue and green with cloud cover. It might survive a passing glance, bit it won't fool any geographers.

Drawing the planet

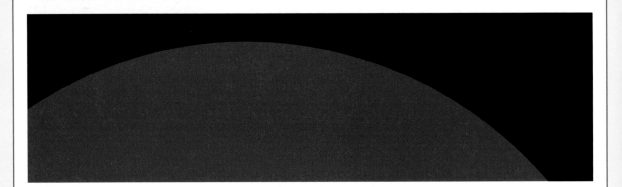

1 Drawing the initial shape should be simple – after all, what could be easier than drawing a circle with the **Elliptical Marquee tool**[4]. But this is a very big circle, and most of it is outside the image area. The trick is to hold two modifier keys before you start to draw: ⌥ *alt* to draw from the center out, and *Shift* to constrain the shape to a perfect circle. While dragging, hold the Spacebar to move the circle around, then release it to keep dragging for a larger shape.

2 I've drawn some land masses on a new layer using a hard-edged **Brush**. Georgraphy was never my strong point at school, and I think it shows. Nevertheless, we'll end up with an earthlike planet; by the time we've added some shading and cloud cover no-one will be any the wiser. (I hope my old Geography teacher isn't reading this.)

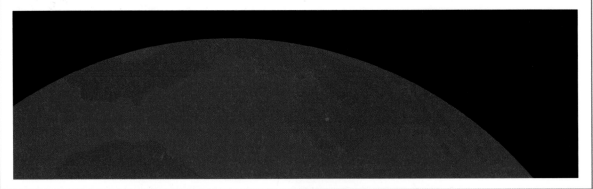

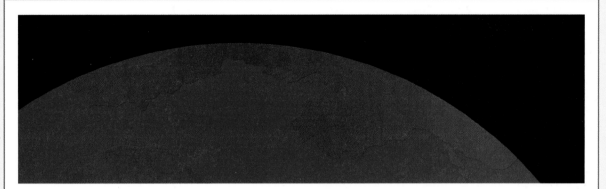

3 To make the basic texture, we'll use – you've guessed it – the **Clouds** filter. Press ⬛ to lock the transparency of the layer first, or the filter will flood the whole image; then, with the foreground and background colors set to brown and green, choose **Filter > Render > Clouds**.

4 To bring a little texture in, I decided to brighten the coastline. Load up the land layer as a selection[6], then use **Select > Modify > Feather**[4] to soften the edges. Switch to the original planet layer, and brighten the selection.

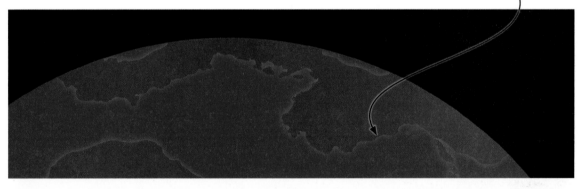

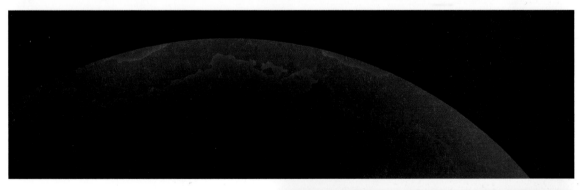

5 Use the **Burn tool** to add some deep shading toward the corner, away from the light source. You may prefer to paint this on a new layer, using the planet as a clipping layer.

6 I've painted some tiny lights in the shadow areas, repurposing the stars **Brush** we created earlier. They're barely visible, but I know they're there.

Painting the silver lining

The way to make our planet look more earth-like is to give it an atmosphere. And the easiest way of creating atmosphere is by adding some cloud cover.

We'll start off by using a technique we've already employed in this chapter to make the basic cloud effect.

Creating the clouds

1 To make the clouds, we're going to use… the **Clouds** filter! I think this is the only time I've ever used this filter for making clouds. The procedure is the same as for Mars: apply the filter to an ellipse, then **Spherize** (far right).

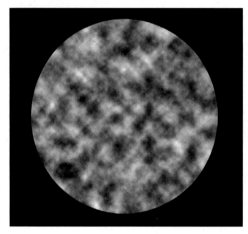
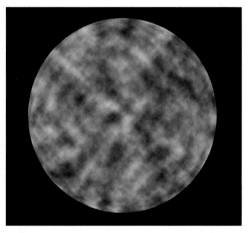

2 We don't need to create the initial Cloud layer very large, despite the size of the planet. There are two reasons for this: firstly, because a texture such as this is so wispy it can be scaled to just about any size without loss of quality. Secondly, the filter always creates small, tight knots of texture. By making it small and then enlarging it, we can expand that texture until it's a size that's more appropriate for the scale of our planet. Here, I've reduced the opacity to 50% so we can see the planet beneath.

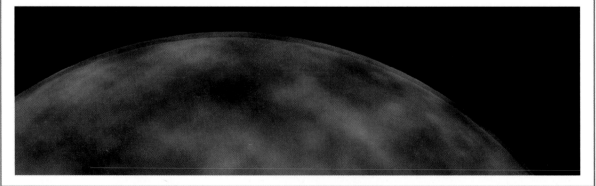

Refining the atmosphere

3 Changing the mode of the cloud layer from **Normal** to **Screen** means it only has a brightening effect on the layer beneath, rather than the black areas darkening it.

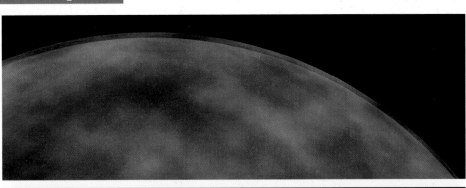

4 The cloud layer was stretched to be slightly larger than the planet, to ensure a complete overlap; selecting the planet area and deleting the cloud outside it means we're guaranteed a perfect fit.

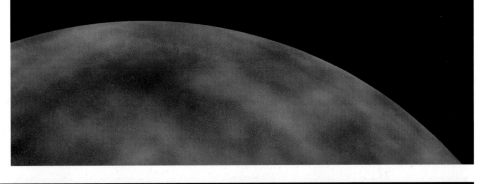

5 When we use the **Brightness/Contrast** adjustment [10] to add contrast to the clouds, they form more convincingly into the sort of cloud cover we expect to see from space (above).

6 Finally, we can add a faint glow around the edge of our planet using the **Outer Glow** section of the **Layer Style** dialog (below). Planet Earth(ish) is now ready for occupation.

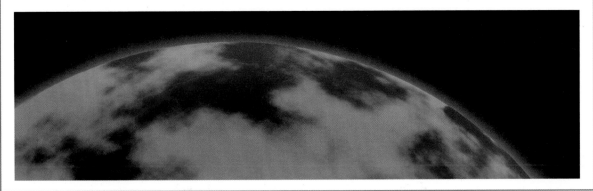

Drawing down the sun

We're two planets ahead now, so knocking up a quick Sun shouldn't be too much of a problem.

The interesting part here is creating the random radiating rays. It's a process that takes several steps, but when finished will leave you with a starburst effect you can use again and again.

Shape, color and texture

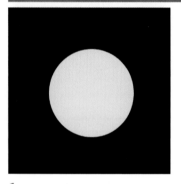

1 We start with a simple circle, filled with yellow. This is a good base color that we can build on later.

2 With the foreground still set to yellow, set the background color to white and… yes, it's the **Clouds** filter once again.

3 To make the sun dazzle, make a new layer and pick a large, soft-edged brush. A single dab of white should be enough to create the glowing effect.

4 To make a convincing outer glow, duplicate the original Sun layer. We could just paint a yellow circle, but this is a better method: choose **Filter > Blur > Radial Blur**, and choose **Zoom** as the blur method. This creates a particularly pleasing glow effect that's much softer than we could achieve with a brush alone.

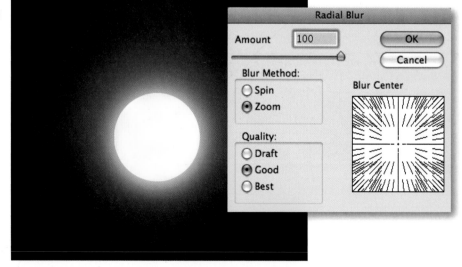

Radial Blur

Amount   100   OK

Cancel

Blur Method:
○ Spin
◉ Zoom

Blur Center

Quality:
○ Draft
◉ Good
○ Best

Radiating those rays

5 Make a new, perfectly square document. Down the center, on a new layer, paint some black and gray blobs of varying sizes.

6 Paint between the blobs at a low opacity, so that there are no white gaps left between them. Make sure you paint all the way to the edge of the canvas.

7 Choose **Filter > Stylize > Wind**, set the method to **Blast**, and set the direction to **From the Right**. this produces the ragged-edge effect seen here.

8 Now repeat the **Wind** filter once more, this time setting the direction to **From the Left** to apply the effect to the other side.

9 Rotate the layer 90°, and move it to the center of the document; use **Free Transform**[6] to scale it so it takes up rather over half the total height of the canvas.

10 Apply **Filter > Distort > Polar Coordinates**, making sure the **Rectangular to Polar** option is checked. This filter wraps the image around a circle.

11 Now apply **Filter > Blur > Radial Blur** once more, with a Blur Method of **Zoom**, to soften the ray effect. We end up with an appealing set of radial rays.

12 With the rays complete, we can drag them back into our original document, tint them yellow and place them on top of the sun for an attractive burst effect.

A couple of points of interest: we made the rays in black, rather than yellow, simply so that we could see them in the new document. It's easy enough to change their color afterwards, but it can be hellishly difficult to see what's going on when we create them in yellow.

It's important to make sure the document is truly square in step 5: otherwise, the Polar Coordinates filter will produce an elliptical effect, rather than one that's exactly circular.

Building the cosmos

Stars and planets are all very well in themselves, but to make space look really *spacey* we need some additional texture and substance.

Creating these two different galaxies is very easy, but the effect they have on the final image can be dramatic.

The first galaxy

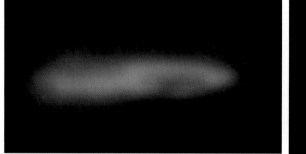

1 Start by painting a few blobs of white on a new layer. This doesn't have to be large, as we'll stretch it later (above left).

2 It's the **Clouds** filter again. Lock the transparency with the ⬛/ key to avoid filling the whole image (above right).

3 All we have to do now is stretch the whole thing to fill, rotating to make an appealing galaxy (below).

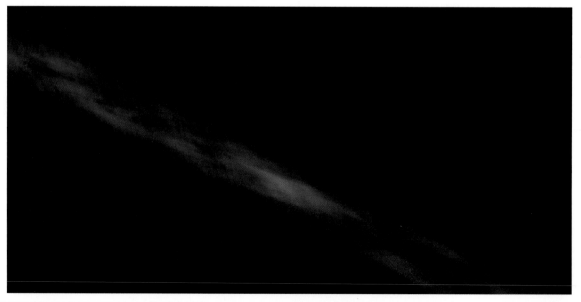

The Milky Way

4 We can make the spiral Milky Way effect in a similar way to the galaxy, first painting with a soft brush on a new layer. This time, try to make the center thicker than the ends, as they will form the arms of the spiral and need to have some body to them.

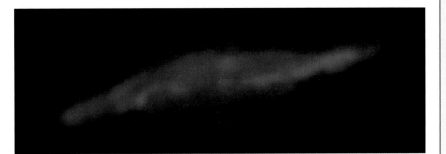

5 I'm not going to tell you which filter we use on this layer. But be sure to lock the transparency of the layer first, or the whole image will be flooded with clouds. Oops! It just slipped out.

6 To make the spiral effect, make a selection centered around the layer you've just created. Use **Filter > Distort > Twirl** to spin the shape into a Milky Way format. You won't see much in the tiny preview window while using this filter, so guess an appropriate twirl angle; I used 200° to create this simple spinning effect.

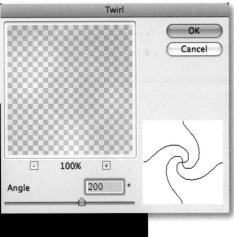

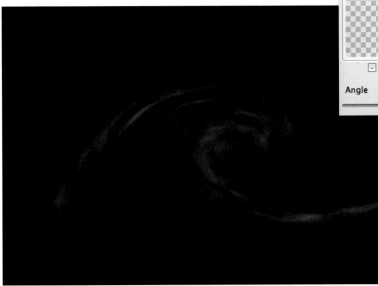

The flying saucer

Although we could leave our new solar system empty of life, it always helps to add the human element – or, in this case, the inhuman element.

The four flying saucers that complete this image are easily drawn directly in Photoshop; as is so often the case, it's the lighting that makes them come to life.

The basic shape

1 Begin by making a circular selection on a new layer, and fill with gray. No **Clouds** filter this time: instead, use **Dodge** and **Burn** to add some texture.

2 To make the smaller disk, duplicate the original. Enter **Free Transform** mode and hold ⌥ Shift / alt Shift to scale proportionally from the center.

Simple transformation

3 Creating a circular array is straightforward. On a new layer, draw one circle and drag a copy of it straight down – clockwise, the 12 and 6 positions.

4 Duplicate the layer; use ⌘ T / ctrl T to enter **Free Transform**, then hold Shift as you rotate. The rotation will snap to 15° angles; stop when you perform a 90° rotation.

5 Merge the two previous layers together, then duplicate and **Free Transform** twice more, rotating 30° each time, to make the new positions.

6 Finally, merge all the layers of the light holes together, and merge them all down into the saucer base.

Perspective and depth

7 Use **Free Transform** to squeeze the saucer vertically. Then hold ⌘ ⌥ Shift / ctrl alt Shift as you drag a corner handle horizontally to add perspective: this makes the far lights closer together than the front lights, improving the perspective appearance.

8 Hold ⌘ ctrl and click on the saucer's name in the **Layers Panel** to load it as a selection. Hold ⌥ alt and nudge down with the cursor keys four or five times to extrude the saucer vertically, adding depth to the edge of the rim.

9 Inverse the selection using ⌘ Shift I / ctrl Shift I, and lock the layer's transparency by pressing /. Fill the rim with a mid gray, and use **Dodge** and **Burn**[12] to add highlights and shadow.

10 To add extra interest, make a copy of the saucer layer and move it behind; then scale it slightly and raise it up to add an additional rim above the original saucer.

Glass and light

11 To make the glass dome, make an elliptical selection on a new layer behind the saucer, and then use a soft-edged brush at a low opacity to paint a faint white glow.

12 With the glass ellipse still selected, hold ⌥ Shift / alt Shift as you drag a larger, lower ellipse to select just the bottom half of the dome. Fill with gray, and shade using **Dodge** and **Burn**.

 **13** Make a new layer for the light. Make a rectangular selection, and add an elliptical top (selection shown in red, left). Soften the edges using **Select > Modify > Feather**[4]. Use the **Gradient tool**, set to **White** to **Transparent**, and drag vertically to make the light beam (right).

14 Move the light on top of the saucer, using **Free Transform** to distort it into a cone shape.

15 Duplicate the lights around the saucer, scaling them down as they recede into the distance.

Shade and color

1 To give the saucer more depth and mystery, we can turn to the **Curves** dialog[8].

First, drag down on the **RGB** curve to darken the whole assembly.

Then switch to the **Green** channel using the pop-up menu at the top of the dialog, and raise the curve very slightly; repeat this process with the **Blue** channel.

It may take a little going back and forth between the Green and Blue channels to get the effect exactly right: we're looking for a deep, gunmetal blue.

Make sure the downward lights are not part of the saucer layer – we don't want to darken or tint them.

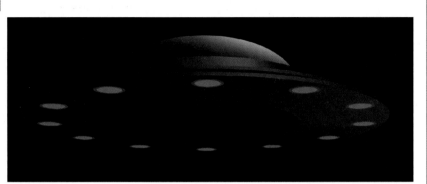

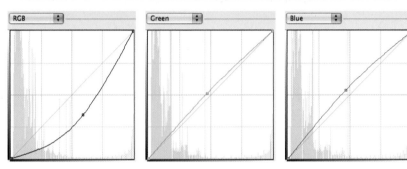

RGB　　　　　Green　　　　　Blue

Duplicating the saucers

2 We can make our single saucer into four by merging the saucer with the lights, then duplicating and scaling them so that they appear to recede into the distance.

But this results in an artificial, duplicated look.

3 The problem is easily solved by rotating the duplicated saucers slightly. Even a small amount of rotation is sufficient to make them all look different.

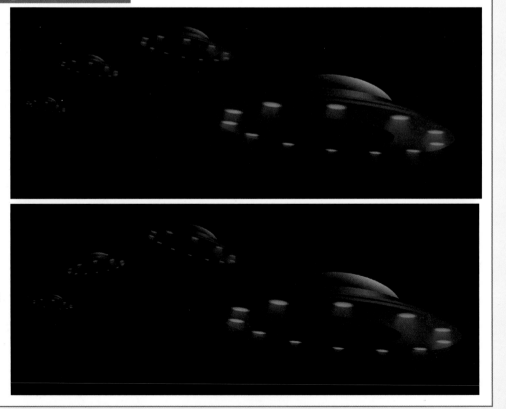

Blending into the scene

4 When we view the saucers against our star and galaxy background, the duplicated versions start to look too dark. Brighten them using the **Curves** or **Levels** dialog for a more realistic appearance.

The final saucer

5 A large saucer in the top right helps the composition and perspective of the scene. Using **Gaussian Blur** [23] to soften it gives it the impression of being much closer to us, as if it's too near to focus on properly.

6 The big saucer is very close to us, and it would seem natural to place it right at the top of the layer stack. But we achieve a far more realistic effect if we move it *behind* the sun layers, so that the sun's glare appears in front of it. This is a useful trick when working with light sources.

The desk drawer

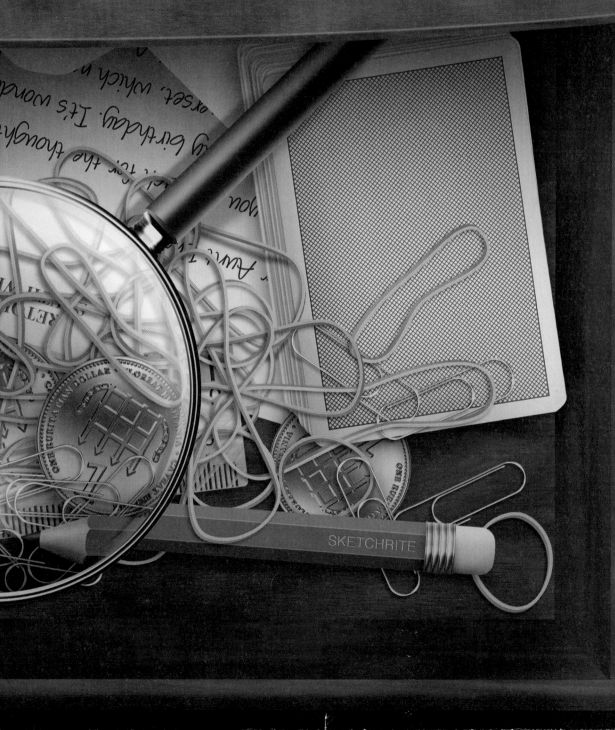

Making the drawer

We'll build this entire piece of furniture out of the wood texture we made on page 24. Increase the contrast[8] and saturation[11] to get a glossy, highly polished look: we want this drawer to appear to be part of a well looked-after piece of antique furniture.

On the following pages we'll look at how to make all the contents of the drawer, before putting it all together at the end.

The drawer tops

1 We can make the top of the drawer front from a thin piece of our wood. Make a rectangular selection, and add a narrow ellipse at each end to round off the edges.

2 Duplicate the layer, and rotate 90 degrees to make the sides. It's worth offsetting the sides before cutting them to length, so they don't look too symmetrical.

The drawer sides

3 Take another piece of the wood texture and darken it, then place it alongside one of the tops already drawn. Use the **Lasso tool** to cut the side at a sloping angle: hold ⌥ *alt* to access the **Polygonal Lasso tool** temporarily.

4 Duplicate the side and flip horizontally to make the opposite side. Darken this one up even more, as this will be the side facing away from the light.

5 Use a rectangular section of the wood texture, and use **Free Transform** to distort it to make the front of the drawer: hold ⌘ ⌥ *Shift* *ctrl* *alt* *Shift* as you drag a corner handle to create the perspective effect.

The base and tabletop

6 Use a large chunk of wood texture to make the drawer bottom. This is typically made of cheaper wood than the visible parts: we can simulate this effect by desaturating it, so it loses some of its gloss. I've also darkened it a lot to make the objects stand out once we place them inside.

7 To make the table top, take a section of wood and flip a copy horizontally to make a symmetrical pattern. This is typical of veneer designs used on old furniture. Use the **Elliptical Marquee**[4] to select a curve for the front, then inverse and delete.

8 Duplicate a section of the front and darken it to make the 'wall' of the table top. Then select the table top and add a white stroke at a low opacity just to the front edge, making a highlight that will add realism.

9 Make a new layer beneath the table top layers. Load up the layers of the drawer as a selection[6] by holding ⌘ Shift ctrl Shift and clicking on each of their thumbnails in the **Layers Panel** in turn: each time you click, that layer's pixel area will be added to the selection. Paint within this selected area with a large, soft-edged brush, at low opacity, to build up the shadow in small stages.

Drawing the iPod

Few everyday objects achieve instant iconic status, but the iPod has managed that feat. Not just once, but with each new version – and that really takes some design talent.

We're going to reproduce the version of the iPod Nano that's current at the time of writing this chapter. Because the real object is so well known, it's important to be as accurate as possible – right down to the typography and the symbols used for the progress bar and the battery life.

The basic shape

1 The subtle curve of the corner is a very distinctive shape. Rather than drawing each corner individually, it makes sense just to draw the one and then duplicate it. I've used the **Pen tool** to draw the top left corner, including the slight radius in the corner itself.

2 Copy this corner horizontally to make the full width of the iPod…

3 …then duplicate vertically to make the bottom section…

4 …and then use the **Rectangular Marquee tool** to select and fill in the middle.

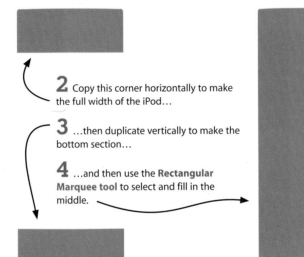

Texture and shading

5 Use **Filter > Noise > Gaussian Noise**[22] to add a little monochromatic noise to the iPod, to add the basic texture.

6 Use the **Burn tool** to add shading to the sides: hold the *Shift* key as you drag to make the shading purely vertical.

7 To make the screen area, duplicate the original iPod shape and fill the copy with black. Reduce it in size so it fits within the iPod area, and shorten the bottom to leave a clear space for the scroll wheel. You may wish to curve the top a little – the easiest way to do this is to use the **Image Warp** controls.

The play triangle

1 Begin by drawing a square, filled with a flat color.

2 Rotate the square 45 degrees to make a diamond shape.

3 Delete half the diamond to make a tall arrow.

4 Use **Free Transform** to compress the arrow to the correct proportions.

The progress bar

1 Make a long white rectangle, then select the left part of it (as much as you want, to indicate the progress) and fill with blue.

2 Select the bottom half of the blue area, and hold **Shift** as you drag horizontally with the **Burn tool** to shade the bottom half.

3 Select the top half of the blue rectangle, and use the **Dodge tool** to brighten it up, again holding **Shift** to drag horizontally.

The battery icon

1 Draw a rectangle with the **Rectangular Marquee tool**, and stroke it with white.

2 Draw a smaller rectangle, again stroked with white, for the battery cap.

3 Select a smaller rectangle inside the first and fill with white to show the current state of the battery.

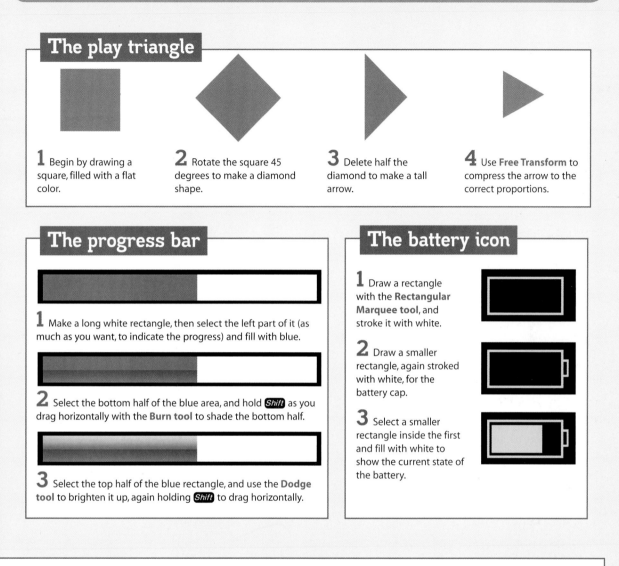

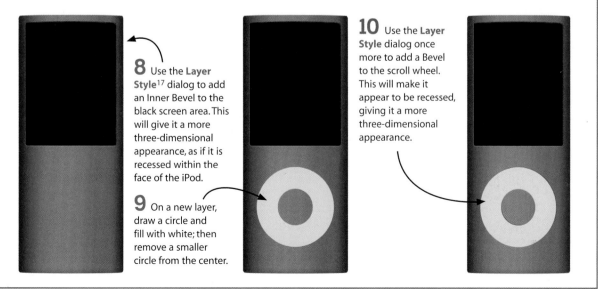

8 Use the **Layer Style**[17] dialog to add an Inner Bevel to the black screen area. This will give it a more three-dimensional appearance, as if it is recessed within the face of the iPod.

9 On a new layer, draw a circle and fill with white; then remove a smaller circle from the center.

10 Use the **Layer Style** dialog once more to add a Bevel to the scroll wheel. This will make it appear to be recessed, giving it a more three-dimensional appearance.

Finishing the iPod

1 Add the triangles we drew earlier, and draw pause lines. Add the MENU text.

2 Color the iPod using **Hue/Saturation**. iPods come in several colors – pick one!

3 Make a smaller copy of the black screen, and add the progress bar and battery icon.

4 Add the image of your choice. I've used the Space image from Chapter 3.

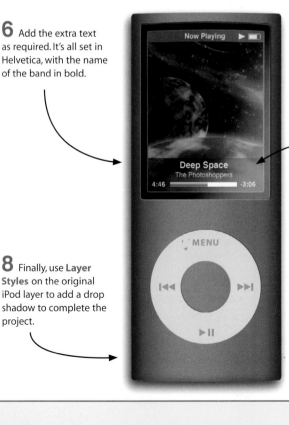

6 Add the extra text as required. It's all set in Helvetica, with the name of the band in bold.

7 Make a new layer, and load up the screen area by holding ⌘ *ctrl* and clicking on its thumbnail in the **Layers Panel**. With a large soft-edged brush, paint the corner in white to add a shine effect.

8 Finally, use **Layer Styles** on the original iPod layer to add a drop shadow to complete the project.

5 Add a black rectangle at the bottom of the image, and reduce the opacity to around 50% to make it translucent.

Movie theater ticket

Compared to the iPod, the movie theater ticket is a very easy object to create.

I've gone for the kind of old-fashioned ticket that used to be handed out years ago, rather than the modern, antiseptic computer-printed tickets we get today.

Creating the coarse paper texture is surprisingly easy, and there's a useful technique for rendering the faded text effect in the final stage.

Drawing the ticket

1 Start by drawing a rectangle, filled with gray. Use the **Elliptical Marquee tool** to select and then delete a semicircle on each side of the ticket.

2 We need to give the impression that the ticket has been torn off a perforated roll. Using the **Smudge tool**, with a very small brush size, smear out tiny scraps of paper at regular intervals all the way down both sides.

3 To make the basic texture, use **Filter > Noise > Gaussian Noise**[22] and add a small amount of monochromatic noise.

4 Lock the transparency of the ticket by pressing **/**, then use **Filter > Blur >Motion Blur**[23] to apply a horizontal blur to the layer. This gives the impression of coarse paper.

Adding detail

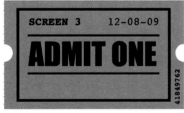

5 Open the **Hue/Saturation** dialog[11], and check the **Colorize** button to add color to the ticket. These tickets tended to come in muted colors – pink, green, blue. Be careful not to oversaturate it.

6 On a new layer, draw the outer rectangle (by adding a stroke to a rectangular selection) and the horizontal lines. I've used the **Courier** font for the date and number, because it looks more like something printed by a machine.

7 Select all the text and border layers, and merge them together using ⌘ E ctrl E. Change the layer mode to **Multiply**, lock the transparency using **/**, and then apply the **Clouds** filter: the white areas will be invisible, making the faded effect in an instant.

Pencil drawing

The pencil is a relatively easy object to draw – and what looks like a complicated business end is actually a series of straightforward, duplicated shapes.

To make the pencil look more real we'll add some scratches to it in the later stages. To make these look like they're really scratched into the surface, we can use a simple Emboss technique that allows us to see the results as we're drawing.

After we've drawn the pencil, it's easy to stretch it to any length we like simply by using Free Transform to make the body longer.

The pencil body

1 Draw a long rectangle on a new layer, filled with mid gray. Then add an elliptical selection to one end to round it off, making the shape that would be left after the tip has been sharpened in a pencil sharpener.

2 Duplicate the shape, and use **Free Transform** to squeeze it to about half its original height. Lighten it, and place the copy above the original shape; then make a second, darker copy, placed at the bottom.

3 Use the **Hue/Saturation** dialog, with the **Colorize** box checked, to add color to the pencil. You may like to use **Brightness/Contrast** afterwards to add greater definition to the upper and lower parts.

4 Switch to the **Brush tool**[5], and choose a small, soft-edged brush. With white as the foreground color, set the tool's pressure to around 30%, and hold *Shift* as you drag horizontally to draw a straight line at the join between the pencil faces. Repeat the process for the other join.

The wooden tip

5 We can use the same piece of wood texture we've used before in this book. Take a small section, and brighten it and lower the contrast to get a faint wooden texture.

6 Use **Free Transform** to create the tip shape: hold *⌘* *⌥* *Shift* *ctrl* *alt* *Shift* as you drag the top left corner down to make the effect.

7 Use the **Dodge and Burn tools**[12] to add shading to make the pencil tip look more rounded.

8 Duplicate the tip layer, shrink it down to make the lead tip, and darken it using **Curves** or **Brightness/Contrast**.

The brass ferrule

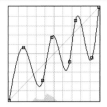

9 Make a thin gray rectangle, and add shading using the **Burn tool**. Copy the layer, and stretch it to make it taller and narrower.

10 Duplicate both sections of the ferrule to make a banded end, then use **Image Warp** or the **Shear filter** to give it a slight curve to the right.

11 Make the metallic effect using **Curves**[16], with a stepped curve similar to the one shown here. Then use **Color Balance** or the **Hue/Saturation** dialog to add some red and yellow for a brassy appearance.

The eraser tip

12 Use the **Shapes tool** to make a fat lozenge with rounded corners.

13 Use the **Dodge and Burn tools** to add shading to the eraser.

14 Add color using the **Hue/Saturation**[11] dialog: keep the saturation level low.

15 Add a little noise using **Filter > Noise > Gaussian Noise**[22].

Completing the pencil

16 Put all the elements of the pencil together. If the wooden tip is behind the pencil body, we'll still be able to see the curved ends of the body. Add a little shading to the body and the eraser beneath the ferrule.

17 To make the scratches, first make a new layer. Open the **Layer Styles** dialog and set a standard **Inner Bevel**, with the direction set to **Down**. Then draw on the pencil with a small hard-edged brush in the same color as the pencil, and the drawn lines will look scratched into the body.

18 The maker's name is simply text set in a color sampled from the brass ferrule. We can copy the Inner Bevel effect from the scratches layer into this one, and it too will appear recessed into the pencil.

SKETCHRITE

The ruler

The only tricky part about making the ruler is getting the tick marks correctly aligned. Remember, you can always make them larger and then shrink them to size – an easier way of making the centimeter and inches scales line up.

Adding the stains and scratches simply adds texture to the wooden surface.

The basic shape

1 Make a ruler shape using the round-cornered **Shapes tool**.

2 Place a piece of standard wood over the top, using ⌘ ⌥ G ctrl alt G to make the shape beneath into a **Clipping Mask**[7].

3 Select the top and bottom thirds of the ruler with the **Rectangular Marquee tool**, apply a 2 pixel feather, and darken so it looks like they're sloping away.

Tick marks

4 Begin with the inches: make seven equally spaced vertical lines.

5 Copy six of the lines, move them halfway along, and shorten them.

6 Repeat the process for the quarter-inch marks…

7 …then repeat it again to make the eighth-inch marks.

8 Making the centimeter ticks is a similar process, except this time we need to make four short lines between all of the half-centimeter tick marks.

9 Type the numbers, and space them out so that they align with the tick marks. You can use *Shift* ⌥ → *Shift* *alt* → to add extra thin spaces between the numbers.

9   5   4   3   2   1   0

0 1 2 3 4 5 6 7 8 9 10 11 12 13 14 15

Stains and scratches

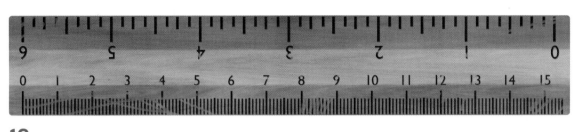

10 Merge all the tick mark and number layers into a single layer, and add a layer mask. Painting on here with a small, hard-edged **Brush** will hide the marks where you paint, producing a convincing impression of scratching. Add a small amount of **Bevel and Emboss** to this layer, to give a recessed look.

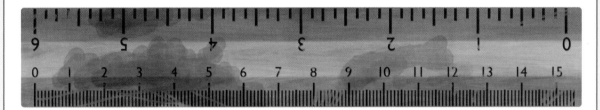

11 To make the stains, first make a new layer and set its mode to **Hard Light**[11]. Using muted reds and blues, paint on the layer at low opacity, building up the effect of ink stains on the surface.

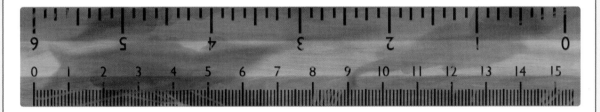

12 Use the **Smudge tool** to smear the stains around the surface of the ruler, stretching and smudging them so they look like they've been there for a long time.

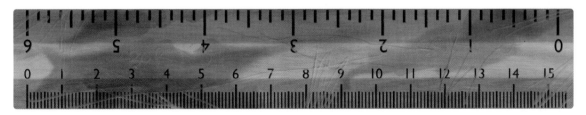

13 To make the scratches, draw on the ruler using a small, hard-edged **Brush**, in a color sampled from the ruler itself. You'll barely be able to see anything – at least, not yet. But when you use the **Layer Style** dialog to add a basic **Bevel** (with the direction set to **Down**), those marks will look as if they have been scratched into the surface.

The pocket watch

Although it looks complicated, the watch is actually a fairly straightforward drawing project. It is a little fiddly in parts, but it can be easily broken down into short, manageable chunks.

Drawing the crown

1 Start by making a small gray circle on a new layer.

2 Make a pattern of vertical black lines on a white background, and use the gray circle as a **Clipping Mask**.

3 Merge the lines into the circle, then select the circle and use **Filter > Distort > Spherize** to create the shape.

4 Lower the contrast on the whole shape, and use **Dodge and Burn** to add a little shading around the edges.

The watch body

7 The post at the top is made from two shaded rectangles. To draw the ring, first draw an ellipse and apply a stroke to it; then copy the **Bevel and Emboss** layer style from the inner ring – hold ⌥ *alt* and drag the style from the inner ring layer onto this one. Use **Free Transform** to squeeze the crown into a compressed shape.

5 Make a gray circle on a new layer. Use the **Bevel and Emboss** layer style to add a three-dimensional effect to it.

6 Duplicate the layer and shrink it slightly to make an edge. On a new layer, draw a stroked circle and apply the same **Bevel and Emboss** effect.

8 Apply the metallic effect as an Adjustment Layer, using **Curves** – use the technique described on page 8.

9 The easiest way to turn the steel look into gold is to use the **Color Balance** adjustment[10]. Add red and yellow until the effect looks right.

10 Make a new white layer for the face. Add a little shading, then make a new smaller white layer and shade with **Dodge and Burn**.

The watch face

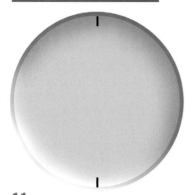

11 On a new layer, make two small black rectangles for the top and bottom tick marks.

12 **Select All**, then use **Free Transform** to rotate the marks. Hold *Shift* to rotate in 30° increments. Press *Enter* to apply the transformation, then use ⌘ ⌥ *Shift* *T* *ctrl* *alt* *Shift* *T* to duplicate the transformation for the new ticks.

13 Repeat the process for the smaller ticks. This time, type in 6° as the rotation angle to make the minute ticks.

14 Draw a circle with the **Shapes tool**, and switch to the **Type tool**: this allows us to type around the edge of the circle. Space the numbers until they fit the tick marks.

15 Draw an inner white circle, and delete a circle from it for the second hand: use **Bevel and Emboss** to add an **Inner Shadow** for a recessed look.

The watch hands

16 Draw half the hand shape with the **Pen tool** and, on a new layer, fill the shape with black.

17 Duplicate the half hand and flip horizontally to make the other half of the hand.

18 Merge the two halves into a single layer, and use the **Elliptical Marquee** to draw a black circle at the bottom.

19 **Bevel and Emboss** adds an **Inner Bevel**. Add a **Drop Shadow**, ticking the **Global angle** checkbox.

Finishing off

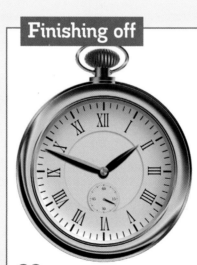

20 The **Global angle** on the drop shadow makes the shadows move with the hands. The center boss is the outer part of the watch, reduced a few times.

21 Tint the watch face pale yellow using **Color Balance**. Make a circular selection on a new layer, and paint glass highlights with a soft-edged brush.

Making the paperclip

The only tricky part of this process is sizing the circles correctly in the first step. We can't simply draw one circle and then shrink it, because the thickness would then be reduced as well.

It may take a little trial and error to get the proportions of the paperclip just right.

The paperclip shape

1 Draw three gray stroked circles, sized so they would fit inside each other. Align the tops of the outer two, and the bottoms of the right two circles.

2 Using the **Rectangular Marquee tool**, select and delete half of each circle as shown here.

3 Use the **Rectangular Marquee tool** again to make selections the width of the circle outlines, and fill to join the ends together as shown.

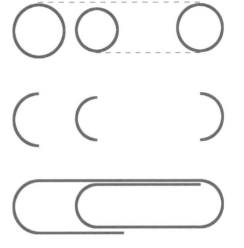

Adding shine

4 Use the **Layer Style** dialog to add an **Inner Bevel** to the paperclip. The settings I've used are a **Depth** of 220%, with a **Size** of 4 pixels and a **Soften** amount of 4 pixels. The gloss comes from the **Gloss Contour** pop-up in the lower half of the dialog, in the **Shading** section.

5 We can add a further shine using the **Satin** section of the **Layer Style** dialog. I've used an **Opacity** of 68%, a **Distance** of 25 pixels, and a **Size** of 29 pixels. Make sure the **Blend Mode** is set to **Hard Light**, click the color swatch and choose a pale blue as the satin color.

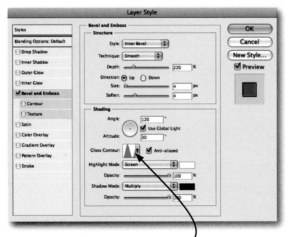

Click the contour button to select an up/down curve from the preset list.

3 Finally, add a **Drop Shadow** to make the paperclip stand out from its background.

Making the elastic bands

This is probably the single easiest object to draw in this book. It uses a useful technique to extrude the flat shapes into three-dimensional forms, though: it's a process that's simple to use but creates 3D objects in next to no time.

Drawing and stroking the shape

1 Use the **Pen tool** to draw a few different elastic band shapes. Even if you're new to this tool, it's a straightforward and easy job.

2 To stroke the path, choose a small, hard-edged brush – around three or four pixels in size – and set a mid gray as the foreground color. When you press the `Enter` key, the path will be stroked with the current painting tool, which in this case is the brush we just selected.

Extruding the bands

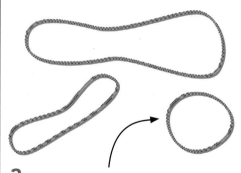

3 Use **Select All** to select the entire layer, and hold the `⌥` `alt` key as you nudge the selection up and left with the cursor keys. Keep nudging with the keys and you'll extrude the elastic bands.

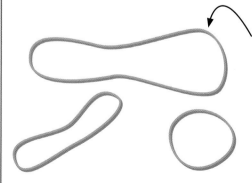

4 With the topmost 'extrusion' still selected, use the **Curves** or the **Levels** adjustment to brighten the upper surface. This makes the remainder of the band look like a real edge. For added realism, use `⌘` `Shift` `I` `ctrl` `Shift` `I` to inverse the selection, and use **Dodge and Burn** to add extra shading.

5 Inverse the selection again so that the original upper surface is selected, make white the foreground color, and use **Edit > Stroke** to apply a 1-pixel stroke at 40% opacity. This makes a neat edge line.

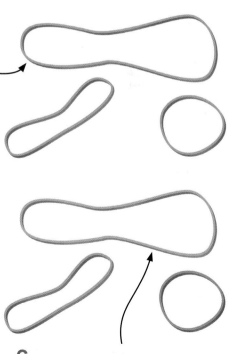

6 You can color the elastic bands using **Color Balance** or **Hue/Saturation**[11]. Pale brown is a good starting color; some bands also come in red, blue, green and yellow.

Playing cards

In this exercise we'll create a simple background pattern for our card backs. We'll add a shadow to each card, then merge the whole stack together and remove the shadow from outside the card stack.

The card shape

1 Use the **Shapes tool** to draw the outline for the card. There are three modes for this tool: it can draw a new **Shapes Layer**, or a **Pen path**, or it can just create a regular layer. It's the last option that we want to use here.

Choose the **Rounded Rectangle** icon from the **Shapes** bar. You'll need to experiment with the **Radius** setting to before you find a corner size that's just right for a playing card. Draw the card on a new layer, in a pale brown color.

Back face texture

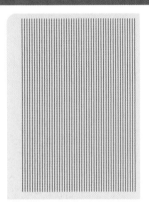

2 Start by drawing a vertical blue line, on a new layer. Select it, then hold ⌥ *alt* as you nudge it with the cursor keys, holding *Shift* as well to nudge it 10 pixels at a time.

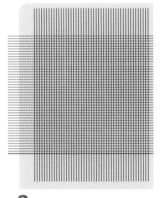

3 Duplicate the lines layer and rotate it 90 degrees to make a regular grid pattern. Merge the two layers together to make a single grid layer.

4 Rotate the grid 45 degrees in either direction…

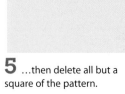

5 …then delete all but a square of the pattern.

6 Duplicate the square of diagonal grid pattern until it fills the surface of the card.

You'll find this much easier if you take the trouble to crop the square accurately in the previous step: try to ensure that the left edge of the pattern square exactly matches the position of the grid on the right edge.

It doesn't matter if the pattern extends off the side or bottom of the card – we can easily cut it down later.

Stacking and shading

7 Cut off any edges of the grid pattern so that it falls within a neat border inside the card. Select the grid area with the **Rectangular Marquee tool**, and use **Edit > Stroke** to apply a blue stroke to the edge.

8 Use the **Layer Styles** dialog to add a **Drop Shadow** to the card. This should be close to the card, and small in size: it's only there to differentiate between each card and the next.

9 Merge the grid into the card to make a single layer. Switch to the **Move tool**, and hold ⌥ *alt* as you drag it to move a copy of the card above the original.

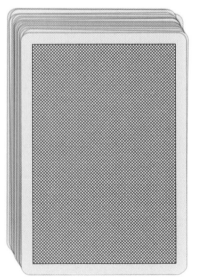

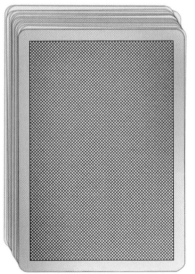

10 Keep creating copies, holding ⌥ *alt* as you drag, until you get a stack of cards. Don't try to be too precise with the placement: the more uneven the stack, the more it will look like a real set of cards. If you like, rotate a couple of them slightly for extra realism.

11 Use the **Burn tool**, set to **Midtones**, to add a little shading to the uppermost card. The aim is to give it a slightly worn, used appearance.

Merge all the cards into a single layer – or hide the background layer and make a **Merged Copy**.

12 We now need to remove the shadow outside the cards. Hold ⌘ *ctrl* and click on the merged layer's thumbnail to load it as a selection, then use ⌘ *Shift* *I* *ctrl* *Shift* *I* to inverse that selection. Press *Backspace* and the shadow will be deleted.

Push the envelope

Building this envelope in Photoshop is surprisingly like building one out of paper: we're working with similar shapes and pieces, and the layer stacking order means we can place our letter inside it.

Once again, we make the object look a little grubby for extra realism.

Front of the envelope

1 Draw half the envelope using the **Pen tool**. This is the only way to get the right shape.

2 Add a blue tint, and use **Filter > Texture > Texturizer** to add a small amount of **Canvas** texture. It's shown here greatly enlarged.

3 Duplicate the envelope and flip horizontally to make the other half.

4 The front flap can be made by placing two half envelope copies together.

Adding shadows

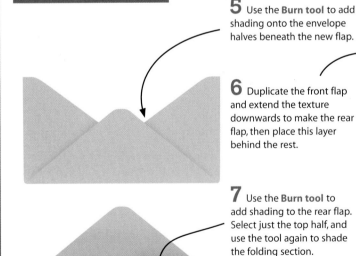

5 Use the **Burn tool** to add shading onto the envelope halves beneath the new flap.

6 Duplicate the front flap and extend the texture downwards to make the rear flap, then place this layer behind the rest.

7 Use the **Burn tool** to add shading to the rear flap. Select just the top half, and use the tool again to shade the folding section.

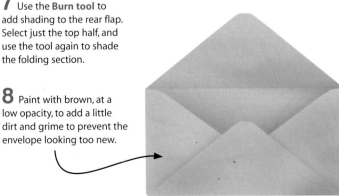

8 Paint with brown, at a low opacity, to add a little dirt and grime to prevent the envelope looking too new.

Creating the letter

9 The letter texture and color is created in exactly the same way as the envelope, using **Filter > Texture > Texturizer**. The handwriting font used here is **Angelina**, a free download from **www.dafont.com**.

10 The address is set in **Times Bold**. To make it look embossed, add a slight **Bevel** using the **Layer Styles** dialog.

Finishing off

11 For a more realistic appearance, we can suggest a gummed area at the edge of the flap. Hold ⌘ *ctrl* and click on the flap's thumbnail in the **Layers Panel** to load up its selection, then, with a selection tool active (but not the **Move tool**), nudge the selection itself down a little way. Inverse the selection using ⌘ *Shift* *I* *ctrl* *Shift* *I* so only the edge of the flap is selected, and use the **Dodge and Burn tools**[12] to paint some highlights and shadows.

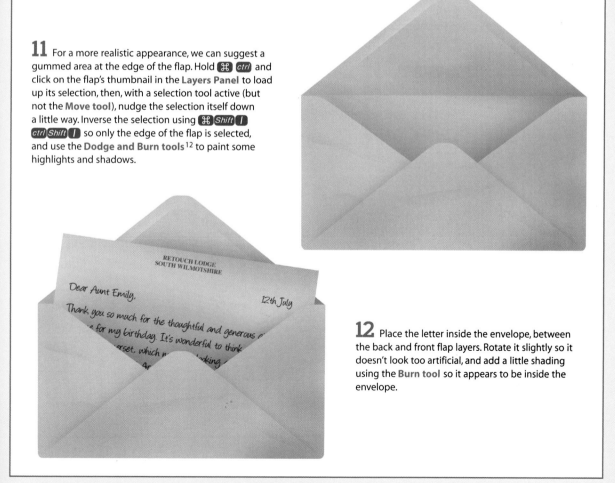

12 Place the letter inside the envelope, between the back and front flap layers. Rotate it slightly so it doesn't look too artificial, and add a little shading using the **Burn tool** so it appears to be inside the envelope.

Coining it

Drawing the coin makes use of the Lighting Effects filter, which creates three-dimensional-looking artwork from a grayscale 'bump map'. We'll begin by creating this bump map as a series of layers, before copying it to a new channel.

Base and perimeter

1 Begin by drawing a pale gray circle on a new layer. This will form the basis of our coin.

2 Select the circle again, and use **Select > Modify > Contract** to shrink it by around 6 pixels. Then add a 4-pixel dark gray **Stroke**, so there's a little pale gray at the edge.

3 Use the **Shapes tool** to draw a circle as a **Path**, then switch to a small hard-edged **Brush**: set the **Spacing** to 300%, and hit *Enter* to stroke the path with the brush.

The portcullis

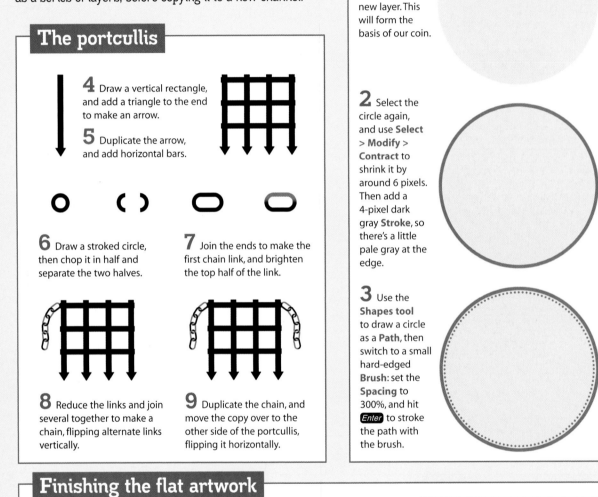

4 Draw a vertical rectangle, and add a triangle to the end to make an arrow.

5 Duplicate the arrow, and add horizontal bars.

6 Draw a stroked circle, then chop it in half and separate the two halves.

7 Join the ends to make the first chain link, and brighten the top half of the link.

8 Reduce the links and join several together to make a chain, flipping alternate links vertically.

9 Duplicate the chain, and move the copy over to the other side of the portcullis, flipping it horizontally.

Finishing the flat artwork

10 To make the circular text, first use the **Shapes tool** to draw a circle as a **Path**. Then move the **Type tool** near the path and, when you click, the text will run around the perimeter of the path. Drag the center marker handle to position the text and to flip it if necessary.

11 Select all, and use ⌘ *Shift* **C** *ctrl* *Shift* **C** to make a **Merged Copy**. Open the **Channels Panel** and make a new channel, then **Paste**. Use **Filter > Blur > Gaussian Blur** to add a 1-pixel blur to the artwork in the new channel.

The Lighting Effects filter

12 Make sure you're viewing the layer, and not the new **channel**, and duplicate the original gray layer at the top of the stack. Choose **Filter > Render > Lighting Effects**.

At the bottom of the Lighting Effects dialog is the **Texture Channel** pop-up menu: choose **Alpha 1**, which will be the new texture channel we created in the previous step.

Uncheck the **White is High** checkbox, and experiment with the sliders until you get an effect similar to the one shown here.

The **Texture Channel** uses the light and dark information to create the 3D effect. Blurring the artwork in the previous step created the thickness of the edge of the text and portcullis: the larger the blur amount, the larger the embossed edge will be.

Drag the handles to shape and position the spotlight

Drag the Intensity and Focus sliders to vary the strength of the effect

Lighting Effects

Style: Default

OK
Save... Delete Cancel

Light Type: Spotlight

☑ On

Intensity: Negative 20 Full

Focus: Narrow 69 Wide

Properties:

Gloss: Matte 0 Shiny

Material: Plastic 69 Metallic

Exposure: Under 0 Over

Ambience: Negative 8 Positive

☑ Preview

Texture Channel: Alpha 1

☐ White is high

Height: Flat 100 Mountainous

Uncheck the White is High box

Choose the Texture Channel in the pop-up menu

Drag the slider to Mountainous for a stronger effect

Shine and color

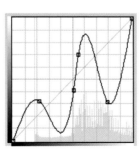

13 The result of the **Lighting Effects** filter was a coin that looked like plastic rather than metal. We can make it metallic using the **Curves**[16] dialog. This is the shape I drew; experiment with different stepping effects on your own artwork.

14 The coin can be colored using **Color Balance**[10] to make a variety of metals. I've added red and a little yellow for a copper look.

Magnifying glass

The magnifying glass uses Layer Styles to create the metallic effect both on the collar and on the glass surround. This is a different method to using Curves to create metal, and it has the advantage that we can control its appearance on the fly, without having to rework an Alpha channel or re-render a filter.

Drawing the handle

1 Start by drawing a black rectangle on a new layer. Use the **Elliptical Marquee tool** to select a narrow ellipse the same height as the rectangle, and copy it to the right hand end.

2 Lock the transparency of the layer, and use a soft-edged brush to paint in white at low opacity along the length of the handle.

3 Repeat, with a smaller brush size, to paint a highlight along the bottom edge of the handle.

Making the collar

4 Draw a tall, thin round-edged rectangle in gray on a new layer. Duplicate to make five copies.

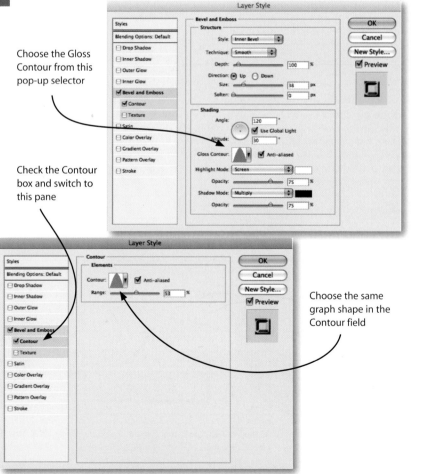

Choose the Gloss Contour from this pop-up selector

Check the Contour box and switch to this pane

5 Open the **Layer Style** dialog and switch to the **Bevel and Emboss** section. Add an **Inner Bevel**, and use the **Gloss Contour** pop-up to choose a curve as shown here. Then check the **Contour** box, and choose the same shape for the contour from the pop-up.

Choose the same graph shape in the Contour field

6 Reduce the middle four shapes, and push them all together so they're touching.

The glass and its holder

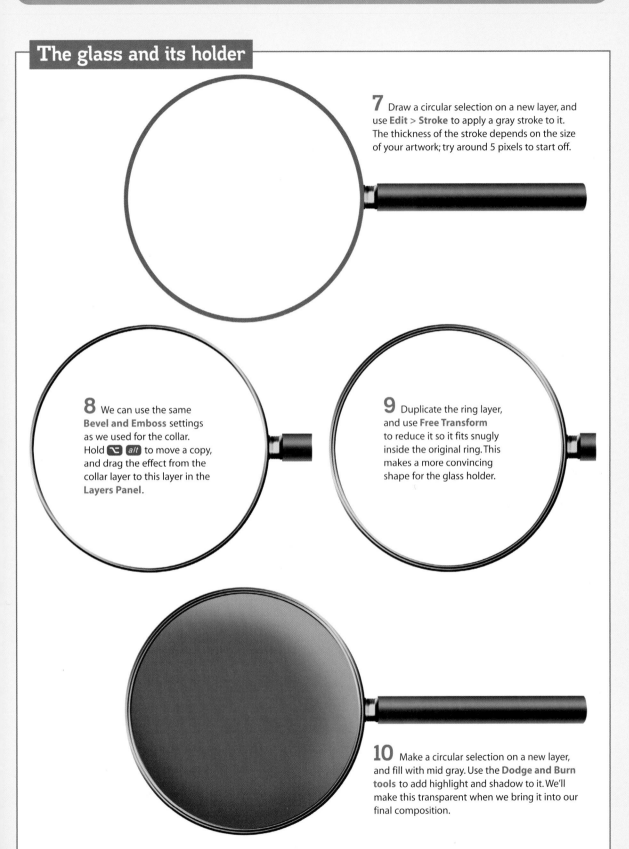

7 Draw a circular selection on a new layer, and use **Edit > Stroke** to apply a gray stroke to it. The thickness of the stroke depends on the size of your artwork; try around 5 pixels to start off.

8 We can use the same **Bevel and Emboss** settings as we used for the collar. Hold ⌥ *alt* to move a copy, and drag the effect from the collar layer to this layer in the **Layers Panel**.

9 Duplicate the ring layer, and use **Free Transform** to reduce it so it fits snugly inside the original ring. This makes a more convincing shape for the glass holder.

10 Make a circular selection on a new layer, and fill with mid gray. Use the **Dodge and Burn tools** to add highlight and shadow to it. We'll make this transparent when we bring it into our final composition.

Glass blowing: the ashtray

The ashtray itself is a fairly simple object; turning it into glass is simply a matter of adding appropriate shading before applying the Plastic Wrap filter.

Changing the layer mode to Hard Light allows us to see through it to the table beneath.

The basic shape

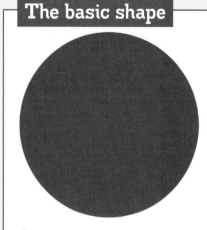

1 Begin by creating a circle, on a new layer, filled with a mid gray color. This is the best tone to use when we're going to apply **Plastic Wrap** later.

2 Hold ⌘ *ctrl* and click on the layer's thumbnail to load its selection. Inverse the selection, feather by about 4 pixels, and brighten the edge.

Adding the detail

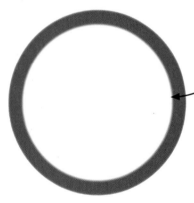

3 Make a smaller circular selection inside the ashtray, feather the edge by around 3 pixels, and fill with white.

4 Each of the indents is a simple shaded rectangle: place them around the perimeter so they project into the center of the ashtray.

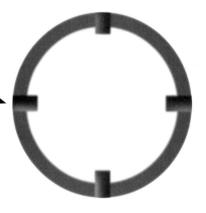

5 Draw another circular selection, slightly smaller than the white one, and fill with a darker gray to make the interior sides of the ashtray.

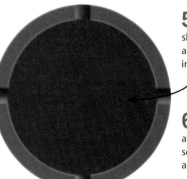

6 To make the bottom of the ashtray, make another, smaller circular selection and darken this so the sides are clearly defined outside it.

Shading and shine

7 Use the **Dodge and Burn tools** to add some random shading to the base of the ashtray. At the same time, add a little variation in the edge to stop it looking so uniform.

8 Use **Filter > Artistic > Plastic Wrap** to create the shine. You get a large preview with this filter, so experiment with the settings until you get a strong glossy result.

The ashtray on the table

9 If you've used several layers to create the ashtray, merge them together and bring them into the table document. Use the **Hue/Saturation** dialog, checking the **Colorize** box, to apply a blue tint to the whole ashtray.

10 When we change the layer mode of the ashtray from **Normal** to **Hard Light**[11] we can see the table texture through it. Note how the blue of the ashtray combines with the brown table to produce this appealing green glass appearance.

11 Make a copy of the ashtray layer, and use **Gaussian Blur**[23] to soften it. With the layer mode still set to **Hard Light**, drag it to one side to create the impression of a tinted shadow on the table beneath the ashtray.

12 Although the shadow looks good on the table, it makes the ashtray itself too strongly colored. Load up the ashtray layer by holding ⌘ *ctrl* and clicking on its thumbnail; then make a **Layer Mask**[7] for the shadow layer and fill the selected area with black to hide it.

Filling the drawer

Now that all the elements have been completed, we can start to fill the drawer. A useful tip is to turn the key objects – the watch, ruler, cards, pencil and so on – into Smart Objects first. That way we can scale and rotate them as much as we like as we experiment with their position, without any loss of quality.

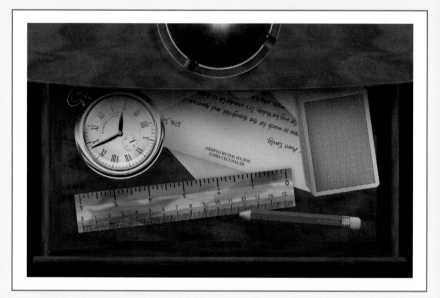

Object shadows

1 The easiest way to add basic shadows is to use a **Layer Style**, setting a standard **Drop Shadow** using **Global Lighting** as the lighting direction. That way, even if the objects are rotated, their shadows will still all point the same way.

2 Setting a drop shadow using **Global Lighting** works especially well on smaller objects, such as the paperclips. Keep each paperclip as a separate layer, and as they're rotated each one will still cast its shadow the right way.

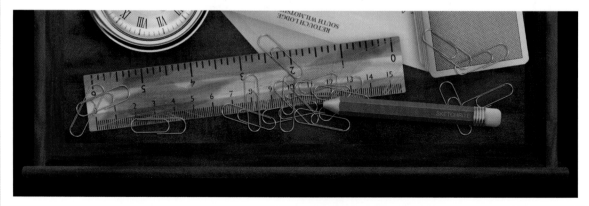

More contents

3 As we add more objects to the drawer, we start to face new positional and shading challenges. The movie theater ticket, for instance, rests on the iPod and is held there by the watch; additional shading can help it to look as if it bends over the top of the iPod, even though the object itself is not distorted.

4 The elastic bands can be moved and copied as a group of three, as we originally drew them: each group can be colored to add variation. When there's so much going on, no-one will ever spot that there are only three variations.

5 The magnifying glass is the only tricky object to work with. As it stands, the glass is still opaque – but if we keep it as a separate layer, we can work on it independently.

The drop shadow here is slightly more complex than could be created with **Layer Styles**. To make this, duplicate all the magnifying glass layers and merge the copies into a single layer. Fill this layer with black, apply a fair amount of **Gaussian Blur** to soften it, and reduce the opacity.

Offset the shadow in the same direction as the rest of the shadows in the composition.

The magnifying effect

6 If we change the mode of the magnifying glass itself from **Normal** to **Hard Light**, we can see through it to the scene beneath. But this still isn't enough: we need to distort the view so that it's enlarged. Not a lot, as the magnifying glass is very close to the objects, but enough to make sense of it as an object.

7 To start, hide the glass layer, and load it up as a selection by holding ⌘ ctrl and clicking on its thumbnail. Use ⌘ Shift C ctrl Shift C to make a **Merged Copy** of the artwork in that selected area – you may need to switch to a visible layer in order to do this, depending on your version of Photoshop. **Paste** the merged copy, then select it again; use **Filter > Distort > Spherize** to add a small spherizing effect – but only around 30% at most. Magnifying glasses don't distort all that much.

8 We need to enlarge the magnified view slightly to make it more imposing. But we don't want it to extend beyond the edges of the lens.

A simple solution is to duplicate the spherized layer, and then use ⌘ ⌥ G ctrl alt G to use the original as a **Clipping Mask**[7]. Now when we enlarge the uppermost, copied layer, it will only be visible where it overlaps the original layer beneath.

Enlarge it enough so that we can see the effect clearly: the ticket, ruler and pencil are here clearly offset from their non-magnified originals.

Finishing the illustration

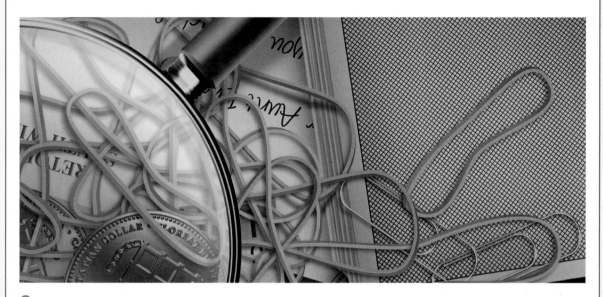

9 Some of the shadows need to be modified to make them bend over objects. We can do this, even though they were created as **Layer Styles:** *ctrl* click / right click on the style's name in the **Layers Panel** and choose **Make Layer** to convert the style to a regular layer. This allows us to select a portion of the shadow and modify it. We can now make the red elastic band shadow bend correctly over the edge of the cards, for instance.

10 Finally, let's add some more dramatic lighting to the scene. On a new layer, use a very large soft brush to paint in brown around the edges of the scene. Set the mode of the new layer to **Hard Light**[11] for a stronger, transparent effect. And that's it – this complex scene is now complete.

CHAPTER 5
Fantasy art

Background texture

In this chapter we'll create a fantasy illustration of a horned devil wielding a handful of shiny, snake-like objects.

Whether or not you want to create this type of scene, the chapter is instructive in that it deals with a variety of ways of making glistening, shiny objects. We'll look at all the techniques involved, starting with the background texture.

Although it may seem like a complex background, it's easy to create using just a few filters and effects.

Difference Clouds

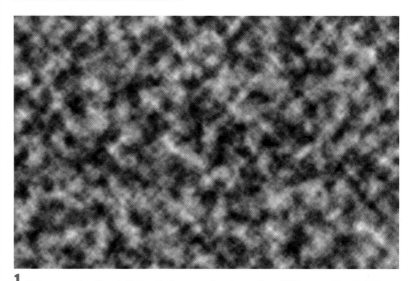

1 We've used the **Clouds**[20] filter before: now, here's a variant, **Difference Clouds**. This filter builds on the previous effect to increase and tighten the effect. Begin by setting the foreground and background colors to black and white, then choose **Filter > Render > Difference Clouds**. This creates a texture similar to the one seen above. Press ⌘ F ctrl F to repeat the filter. Each time, it gets tighter. Two intermediate steps are shown below; the final result is seen at the bottom.

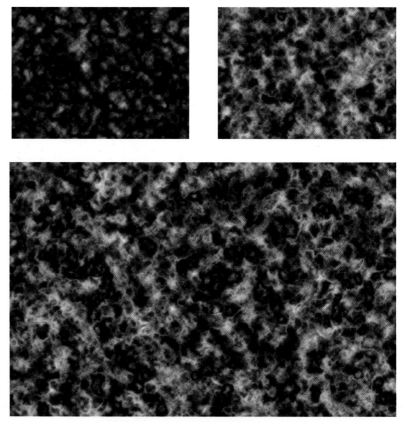

Nose and mouth

4 Click and drag between the eyes, smearing both up and down in several stages to make the shape of the nose. The bottom of the nose can be smeared out to make the nostrils.

5 To make the mouth, pick a dark area once again and smear into shape. As you do so, a lighter, shiny edge will form automatically: this creates the lip effect for you.

6 Continue to smear in the image to make the beard, the shape of the chin, and a suggestion of ears. Once again, it's easy to correct mistakes; the face can be built up using a series of small movements rather than one big smudge, so you can construct it piece by piece until the texture forms itself into the shape of a head.

7 When the face is complete, press the **OK** button to exit the **Liquify** filter. We now need to darken the inside of the eyes and mouth: this is most easily done by simply painting within this area in black. Work on a new layer, if you like, so mistakes can be corrected more easily.

Eyes and teeth

Having made the black space for the eyes and mouth in the previous exercise, it's time to fill them with eyes and teeth.

Neither should pose a significant problem. The trick with the teeth is to get the shape right in the first instance: after that, it's just a matter of shading and color.

Painting eyes

1 We could make realistic eyes for this creature – and drawing eyes is something we'll look at later in the book. But in a face like this, all we really want is a menacing glow.

Either paint the eyes with a soft-edged **Brush**, or make a circular selection and choose **Select > Modify > Feather** to soften it, and fill with red.

Whichever method you choose, work on a new layer so it's then easy to copy it to the other eye.

Shaping the teeth

2 Draw the shape of the teeth on a new layer, using a hard-edged **Brush** in mid gray. Don't worry about the tops of the teeth at this stage – we can make them fit within the mouth later. For now, concentrate on making a convincing set of incisors and molars. Or just make up some fantasy teeth, as I've done here.

3 Use the **Dodge tool**, set to **Highlights**, to paint some bright areas on the bottom and right of the teeth. If you don't use a graphics tablet, it's best to work at a low opacity and build up the effect in small stages.

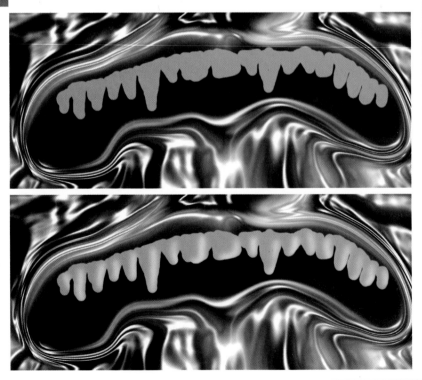

Shading and color

4 Switch to the **Burn tool** and darken the left side of the teeth. If we were going for a realistic look here, we'd use a very small brush to paint between each tooth: but because we're going to darken the whole lot anyway, we don't need to worry about this.

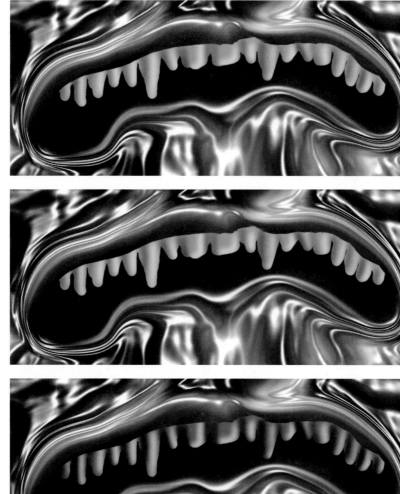

5 To make the teeth fit the mouth, we can simply erase the top. Better, though, to make a **Layer Mask**[7], so we can adjust the shape as we need to. Here, I've drawn the basic shape with the **Pen tool** to guarantee a smooth edge; I've then adjusted it with a hard-edged **Brush** to create a torn scowl.

6 I've used **Color Balance** to apply some blue to these teeth. Again, if we were trying to create a realistic effect, we'd use the same adjustment to add a little red and yellow for a more human appearance.

7 To stop the teeth looking so prominent, darken the whole lot using either the **Curves**[8] or the **Brightness/Contrast**[10] adjustments. The aim should be to make them blend in with the tonal range of the rest of the face.

Drawing horns

The horns are perhaps the most spectacular part of this image. Drawing them makes use of the little-known Transform Again feature in Photoshop, which duplicates the last transformation. It means getting the initial transformation just right, but after that it's a piece of cake.

The initial ellipse

1 Start by drawing a gray ellipse on a new layer. The shape is that of the bottom of the horn, where it meets the head: that's the only consideration at this stage.

2 Use **Dodge and Burn**[12] to add shading around the bottom and left edge. Don't worry about the rest of the ellipse, since it will be hidden in the final image. Add a hotstop on the left for the sake of interest.

Repeated Transformation

3 Duplicate the layer, but don't move it. Use ⌘ T / ctrl T to enter **Free Transform**, and move the ellipse up. Rotate it a couple of degrees clockwise, and scale it to about 90% of its original size – then press **Enter** to apply the transformation.

4 Choose **Edit > Transform > Transform Again**, or (better) use the keyboard shortcut ⌘ Shift T / ctrl Shift T. Keep pressing this key combination a dozen or so times and, each time, a new ellipse layer will appear, moved, scaled and rotated by the same amount.
   The success of this procedure depends on getting the initial transformation just right, so it may take a few tries before the combination of movement, angle and scaling work together well.

5 After half a horn has been drawn, we can cheat the rest. Make a copy of the horn so far and flip it horizontally; then use **Free Transform** again to rotate and scale it so it now curves the other way. Repeat to make the horn curve back on itself, then use the **Transform Again** process to make the horn tip.

Gloss and color

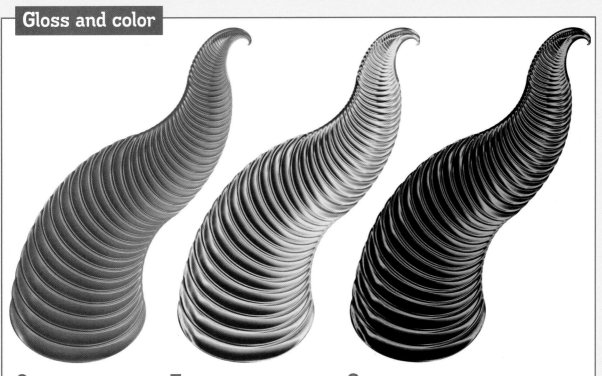

6 To make the horn shiny, begin by applying **Filter > Artistic > Plastic Wrap**. this adds gloss to the shape.

7 We can make the horn shinier still by applying a metallic **Curves** effect to it. See page 16 for details of how to do this.

8 With the shininess now complete, we can color the horn using **Color Balance**, **Curves** or your favorite method. I've also used **Brightness/Contrast** to darken the horn and make it more contrasted.

Onto the head

9 Rotate the horn and place it on top of the head, then duplicate it and flip horizontally to make the other one.

We need to paint out the base of both horns to make them fit behind those enlarged eyes. We can do this with a soft-edged **Eraser**, or, better, make a **Layer Mask**[7] and paint the horns out on that.

Drawing the hand

Although drawing hands is generally one of the more complex tasks in Photoshop, or indeed in any drawing medium, the devilish claw we're creating here is a far simpler proposition.

The key to making this hand work is all in the texture: not only will we apply Plastic Wrap, we'll also smear it for a more vein-like appearance.

The hand shape

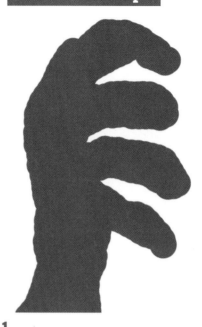

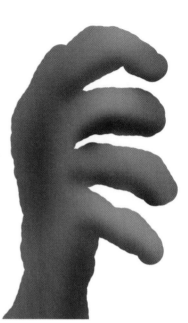

1 Draw the hand shape on a new layer in mid gray, using a hard-edged **Brush**. There's little need for accuracy a this stage – we can fix mistakes later.

2 Use the **Dodge and Burn tools** to add shading to the bottoms of the fingers, as well as a little darkness on the back of the hand.

Shading and texture

3 Use **Dodge and Burn** to add highlights to the upper part of the fingers, and darkness between them.

4 Use **Filter > Artistic > Plastic Wrap** to create an instant shiny effect on the whole hand.

5 Use the **Smudge tool** to smear the highlights down the hand for a more lifelike appearance.

Color and fingernails

6 Tint the hand the same color as the rest of the image and add some contrast to it, as we've done on previous pages in this chapter.

7 Draw the fingernails on a new layer, using a hard-edged **Brush**. Rather than use gray, it can help to draw them in a pale blue sampled from the hand itself.

8 Use **Dodge and Burn** again to darken the underneath of the fingernails, and to add highlights to the top.

9 We can improve the shape of the fingernails by using the **Smudge tool** to smear them back into the hand. This unifies the hand, creating a more convincing appearance.

10 When we place the hand on the background, we can blend it into the image better by using the **Smudge tool** to smear the back a little, removing the hard edge.

Snakes with the Smudge tool

Although we generally think of the Smudge tool as useful for small adjustments only, we can also use it at maximum strength to create twisting, organic forms.

Here, we'll see how a simple blob can be made to create a series of wiggly worms.

Smudging snakes

1 Draw a small round circle, fill with blue, and add shading on the bottom and left. Move this to the bottom of the document, and duplicate the layer.

2 Use the **Smudge tool**, with a hard-edged brush the same size as the blob. Set the **Strength** to **100%**, click in the middle of the blob, and drag up: as you drag, a wiggly shaded shape will be created on the artwork.

3 Take another copy of the blob, and repeat the smudge effect to create another snake.

More snakes

4 Repeat several times to create additional snakes, using a new blob each time.

5 Continue until you have as many snakes as you want.

6 Merge all the snake layers together, and use **Filter > Artistic > Plastic Wrap** to make them shiny.

7 We can repeat with a smaller blob to make thinner snakes.

Finishing off the image

The final step is to add a new color layer so we can bring added interest and life to the picture.

We can add as much or as little color as we like. It can help to duplicate the Color layer, hide the original, and then continue to add color to it until you reach a stage you're happy with.

Painting in color

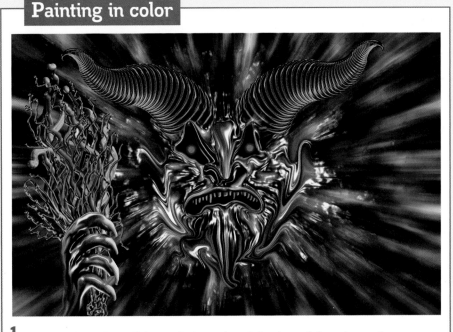

1 Make a new layer, above all the rest. Set its mode to **Color**, then switch to a large, soft-edged **Brush**. Pick colors that suit the scene, and paint over the image. Because of the layer mode, where you paint will color the image translucently. Use a low **Opacity** so you can build the effect up in small stages.

When painting on specific areas, such as the horns and snakes, first load them up as a selection by holding ⌘ ctrl and clicking on the layer's thumbnail in the **Layers Panel**; hold Shift as well to add multiple layers' areas to the selection.

2 You can add as much or as little color as you like. I stopped with the fairly restrained version above, for a more subtle effect; but if you like more color, there's nothing to stop you painting as many shades as you like into the image.

In the attic

In the attic

There's a lot of complicated stuff in this chapter, as well as a few surprisingly straightforward pieces. As always, by breaking the project down into small chunks we can get through it more easily.

We'll begin with shaping the walls for the attic. These not only set the backdrop, they also determine the perspective for this whole scene – so we'll see how to draw vanishing lines and a horizon to help us to make sure that the whole illustration has a consistent, realistic appearance.

Making the walls

1 This is the brick wall we drew on page 26. If it isn't wide enough, duplicate the layer and line the two up; then use a **Layer Mask**[7] to paint out the hard edge, in order to blend the two halves together.

2 Copy a section of the wall to a new layer, and line up along the edge. Enter **Free Transform** and hold ⌘ ⌥ Shift ctrl alt Shift as you drag a corner handle to create the perspective effect.

3 You'll find that every other brick is missing its mortar in the corner, where the two walls meet. Grab a section of mortar from a brick that has some, and copy it to all the bricks that don't.

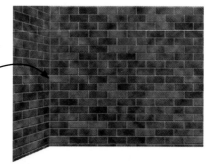

4 The walls need to be darker and less saturated. Use **Hue/Saturation**[11] or **Curves**[8] to do this on the back wall, and then repeat on the left wall, making this one a little darker still.

Adding the grime

5 The brick wall is altogether too clean – but a bit of soot can quickly fix that. Make a new layer, and choose a large **Brush**: set the **Brush** mode to **Dissolve**. Using a low **Opacity**, paint spatters across the wall.

6 When the painting is done, use **Filter > Blur > Gaussian Blur**[23] to apply a 1 pixel radius blur to soften the effect.

Drawing the perspective lines

7 We need to add perspective lines to the scene so we can make everything else match. Use the **Shapes tool**, set to draw pixels, and make a new layer. Set the tool to **Line**, about 4 pixels wide. Draw along the bottom edge of the bricks, from the bottom left inward, continuing past the center of the image.

8 Draw another line from the top left of the brickwork, toward the center. Follow the line of the bricks and continue until the new line crosses the first one.

9 Where the two perspective lines cross is the **Vanishing Point**. A horizontal line, drawn through this point, marks the horizon. You can see how the horizon line matches up with the horizontal line of the bricks on the left wall.

We can use this to make all the perspective in our scene match the view set by the left wall.

Building the rafters

Now that the brick walls have defined the perspective of the scene, we can go on to draw the wooden rafters.

We start by drawing our rafter arrangement flat, as if looking down on it from above. Adding the perspective is straightforward; just remember to make both vertical lines (the sides of the access hatch) point toward the vanishing point as set earlier.

We've got a clever process to add the depth and sides of the rafters, which makes a complex job simple.

The rafter plan

1 We can draw the basic plan of the rafters by drawing a series of parallel gray rectangles, on a new layer. It's easy enough to edit this to add a space for the hatchway.

Adding perspective

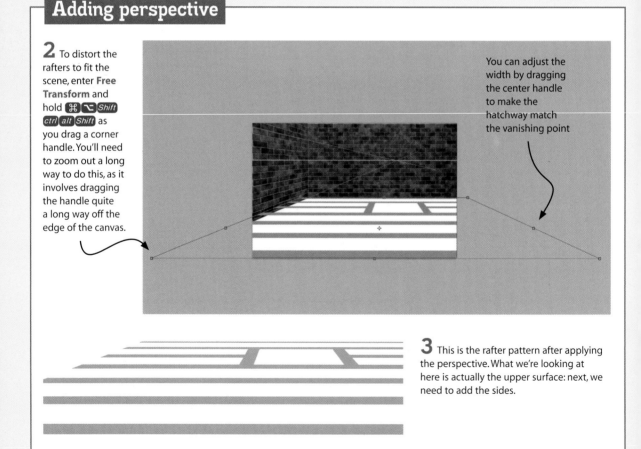

2 To distort the rafters to fit the scene, enter **Free Transform** and hold ⌘ ⌥ *Shift* *ctrl* *alt* *Shift* as you drag a corner handle. You'll need to zoom out a long way to do this, as it involves dragging the handle quite a long way off the edge of the canvas.

You can adjust the width by dragging the center handle to make the hatchway match the vanishing point

3 This is the rafter pattern after applying the perspective. What we're looking at here is actually the upper surface: next, we need to add the sides.

Depth and texture

4 Duplicate the rafter layer, and darken its color; move the duplicated version behind the original in the **Layers Panel**.

This copy marks, in effect, the underneath of the rafters. Move it down to create the depth, and then use **Free Transform** to scale it vertically, adding more depth at the bottom than at the top.

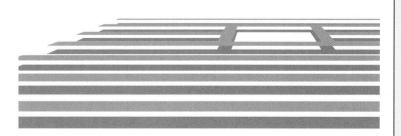

5 Make a series of rectangular selections between the duplicated rafters and the originals, and fill with the same darkened color. We now have the effect of looking at the rafters in true perspective, so we can see their thickness.

6 Because we're going to darken them up considerably, we need to increase the contrast between the top surfaces and the sides. I've done this by brightening the top – the original rafter set.

7 Open the wood texture we created on page 24, and stretch it so that it fills the whole rafter area – use **Free Transform** to add perspective as you do so. Use ⌘ ⌥ G *ctrl* *Shift* G to make a **Clipping Mask** with the rafter layer, and change the mode of the wood layer from **Normal** to **Multiply**.

8 Make thin selections of the edge of the rafters, where the top meets the side, and brighten this edge to make it a little less crisp.

Loft insulation

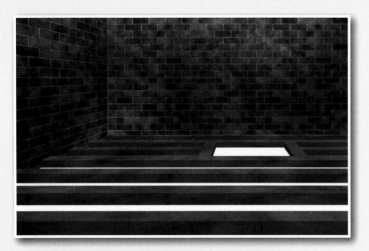

Modern attics have plasterboard nailed to the underside of the rafters; older ones used lath and plaster. We're going to fill in those spaces with rockwool insulation, which is easy to draw and adds texture and interest to the scene.

The first piece of insulation

1 On a new layer, paint a wiggly band of gray. Change the mode of the **Brush** to **Dissolve**, and paint the edges to make this roughened look.

It's only the upper surface we need to worry about; we can mask out the lower surface later.

2 Use **Filter > Blur > Gaussian Blur** to soften the edges slightly. A small blur radius is all that's needed – around 1 pixel.

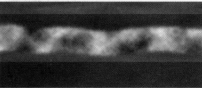

3 Lock the **transparency** of the insulation layer. Set the foreground and background colors to black and white, and use **Filter > Render > Clouds**[20] to add basic texture.

Insulating between all the rafters

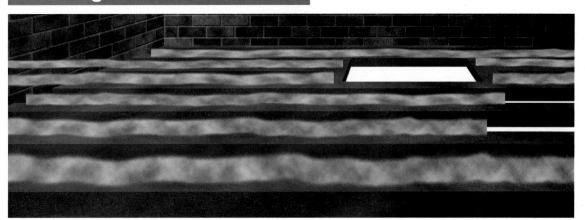

4 Duplicate the insulation layer several times, shrinking each one so that the perspective makes it recede into the distance. As you can see, each piece will now be too narrow to reach all the way to the edges.

5 Merge all the duplicated insulation layers together, then select and drag selections horizontally to fill the gaps left after the previous step.

6 Hold ⌘ ctrl and click on the rafter layer's thumbnail to load it as a selection, then delete the bottom edge of all the insulation so it appears to be nestling between the rafters. I've also darkened it slightly.

The chest of drawers

We can use our trusty wood texture to make the chest of drawers sit in the corner of the attic. The surprisingly easy part of this is drawing the handles, which are far simpler than they look.

We'll begin by drawing just the front of the drawer unit, before taking it into the main illustration to draw the side.

The basic furniture

1 Use the **Shapes tool** to draw a round-cornered rectangle, and fill it with gray. You can draw this as a **Shapes layer**, or as a **Pen path** and then make it into a selection and fill it.

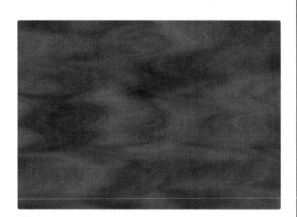

2 Open the wood we drew on page 24, and place it above the shape. Use ⌘ ⌥ G ctrl alt G to make a clipping mask of the original shape, then merge the two layers.

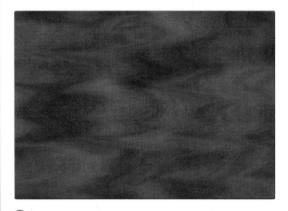

3 Use **Layer Styles**[18] to add a slight **Bevel** to the edge of the resulting layer. This is by far the easiest way to add an instant sense of three-dimensionality.

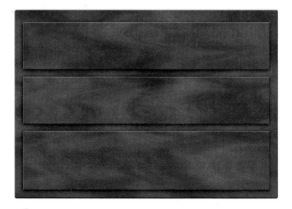

4 Make three rectangular selections and use ⌘ J ctrl J to turn them into a new layer; the bevel will come with them. Add a slight **Drop Shadow**, then flip horizontally to make them appear to be different pieces of wood to the base.

The handles

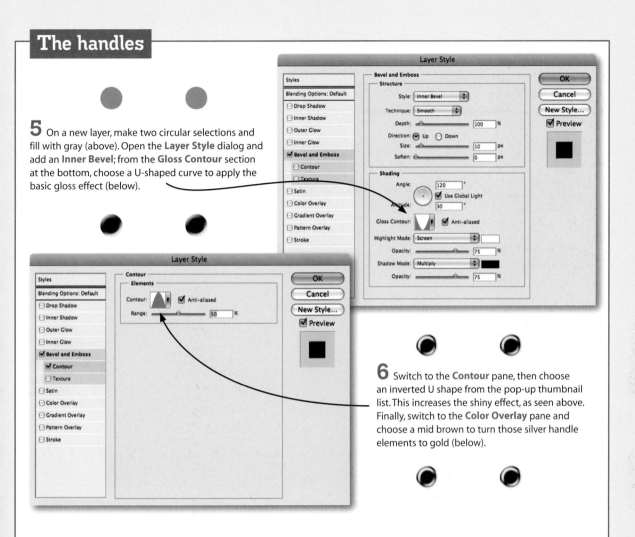

5 On a new layer, make two circular selections and fill with gray (above). Open the **Layer Style** dialog and add an **Inner Bevel**; from the **Gloss Contour** section at the bottom, choose a U-shaped curve to apply the basic gloss effect (below).

6 Switch to the **Contour** pane, then choose an inverted U shape from the pop-up thumbnail list. This increases the shiny effect, as seen above. Finally, switch to the **Color Overlay** pane and choose a mid brown to turn those silver handle elements to gold (below).

7 The handle is drawn in flat gray on a new layer. For ease of drawing, make just one half and then flip a copy horizontally to make a symmetrical handle.

8 Hold ⌥ *alt* and drag the **Layer Style** from the handle base layer that we made above onto this one. All that flat gray will turn to gleaming gold. Add a **Drop Shadow** for added depth.

9 Duplicate the original circular handle bases, move them above the handle, and reduce each one to make the top of the handle holder.

10 Duplicate the whole handle assembly five times – you can merge the layers together if you wish, and all the gold effects and shadows will be retained. The handles finish off the face of the chest of drawers nicely.

Adding the legs

1 Draw a curved leg on a new layer, and flip a copy horizontally to make the other half.

   The leg is most easily drawn with the **Pen tool**, but if you have trouble with that tool (and a lot of people do) you could create it by first drawing an ellipse; then remove rectangular chunks from it with the **Rectangular Marquee tool**.

2 Place a piece of wood texture on top and make a **Clipping Mask** with the leg layer, then merge the two and move beneath the drawers.

3 Add some strong shading using the **Burn tool** to make the legs look as if they're placed just behind the face of the chest of drawers.

Building the side

4 Position the chest of drawers within the scene. Here, I've placed it so that the front legs sit on the third rafter in from the back. I've also rotated the middle drawer slightly, to make it look a little battered.

5 Copy the front and distort it in perspective to make the side. The top and bottom should both point towards the vanishing point.

Completing the legs

6 Now that the perspective of the chest is set, we can go on to draw the sides of the legs. Begin by duplicating the legs layer: move this behind the original legs, and drag it slightly to the right and slightly up, to follow the angle of perspective.

There will be a tiny gap right at the base of the legs. The easiest way to fix this is to use the **Clone tool** to clone in some leg texture, then use the **Eraser** to remove any stray texture.

Finish by darkening the new leg side, and merge with the leg front.

7 Duplicate the leg assembly and make a slightly smaller copy to make the back legs. Arrange them so they sit on the rafter at the back of the attic.

Distressing and varnishing

8 To make the chest look old and battered, we need to add some stains and scratches to it. The scratches are added using the **Hard Light/Bevel** process we used for the ruler, described on page 80.

9 I darkened the chest with a **Curves Adjustment Layer**[8] so it fitted the attic environment better. But it's your choice.

The draped sheet

Although the sheet looks complex, it's not that difficult to draw. It all depends on sensitive use of the Smudge tool: that's how the illusion of folds and wrinkles are created.

The shadow helps to place it in the scene, as is always the case. The slight transparency added at the end gives us a faint view of the handle beneath, which also adds realism.

Basic light and shade

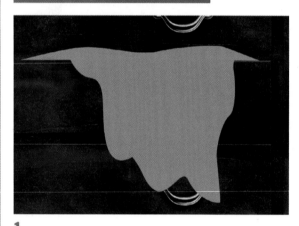

1 Draw the outline of the sheet and fill with light gray. Try to simulate the way fabric would cascade from the drawer.

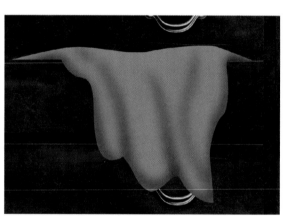

2 Use the **Burn tool** to add shadows beneath the main folds. It only needs to be roughly sketched in at this stage.

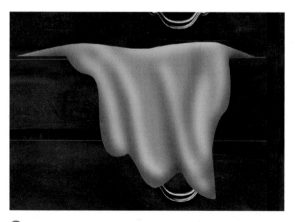

3 Switch to the **Dodge tool** and paint bright streaks next to the dark ones. This forms the basis of the effect.

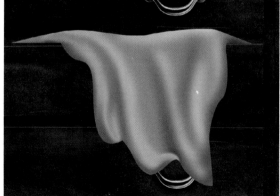

4 Lock the **transparency** of the layer [6], and use the **Smudge tool**, with a soft edged **Brush** and an **Opacity** of around 80%, to smear the shading to follow the shape of the fabric.

Refining the shading

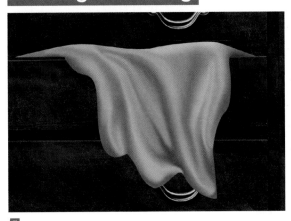

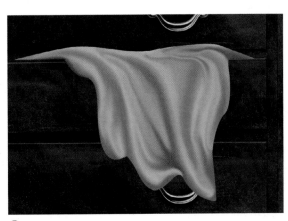

5 Continue to smear with the **Smudge tool**, pushing the light and shade in the direction that the fabric lies. You can add folds by starting to smear from within a dark area.

6 Keep smearing the fabric until the effect looks convincing. You can't really make a mistake here; it's always possible to continue to smudge until the desired effect is achieved.

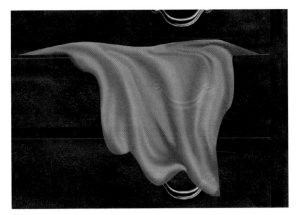

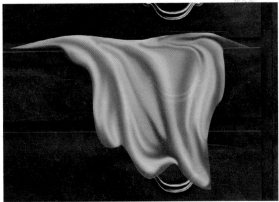

7 Change the **Opacity** of the sheet layer to around **90%**, so we can just see through it to the drawer beneath.

8 Duplicate the sheet layer, and set the mode to **Hard Light**: this strengthens and boosts the whole appearance.

9 Finally, load up the sheet layer as a selection by holding ⌘ ctrl and clicking on its thumbnail. Use **Select > Modify > Feather** to soften the selection by around 8 pixels, and then make a new layer and fill the selection with black.

Move this new shadow layer behind the two sheet layers (the original and the Hard Light version), and offset it to the side. Lower the opacity of the shadow to about 80% so we can see the drawers through it.

The cardboard box

The box needs to be built in perspective, following the horizon and vanishing point we set up earlier. The key here is knowing how much of the inside of the box we can see. Because it's placed below the horizon, we can see inside it.

We'll start by creating the texture for both the sides and the tearaway interior.

Exterior texture

1 Start with a plain gray rectangle. Using two shades of gray, run **Filter > Render > Clouds** to create a subtle mottling effect.

2 Change the color to pale brown using **Hue/Saturation** or **Curves**. We want a light color, as we'll add dark stripes next.

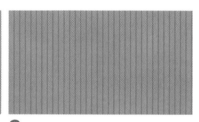

3 Make an array of thin vertical lines on a new layer. The color doesn't matter at this stage.

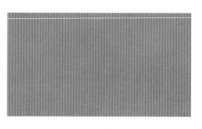

4 Change the layer mode to **Diffuse** to wiggle the lines, and then change the color to a darker version of the brown.

5 Duplicate all the lines to make a finer line array to complete the outside of the box texture.

Interior texture

6 Take a new version of the texture created in step 2; then, on a new layer, paint dark brown vertical stripes.

7 Merge the two layers together, and add some **Noise**[22] to make a rougher cardboard texture.

8 Use a small amount of **Gaussian Blur** to soften the hard noise slightly. This completes the inner texture.

Exterior texture

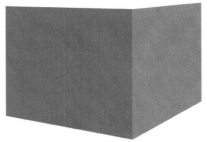

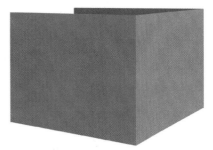

9 Copy the exterior texture layer, and distort it in perspective to make the front face of the box.

10 Duplicate this layer, flip horizontally and apply more perspective distortion to make the side. Then return to the front face, and add some shading to darken it up.

11 Duplicate the front face, darken it, and move it behind the other two. Use **Free Transform** again to reduce it in size so it makes the interior of the box.

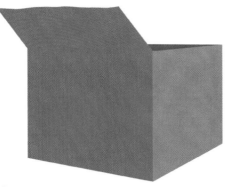

12 Take a section of the front, and distort it to make the front flap. Use the **Lasso tool** to cut away a wiggly top edge as if it has been torn open.

13 Add some shading to the lower half of this flap to differentiate it from the front of the box.

14 Duplicate the flap, and place the copy behind. Fill with a darker brown, and add some noise to give it texture. Then take a section of the box front and rotate it, using the flap copy as a **Clipping Mask** [7], and darken to make the right side of the thickness of the flap.

15 Repeat the previous processes to make the flap on the far side of the box. The basic box model is now complete.

Scotch tape

16 Draw the tape on a new layer, and fill with gray. Use **Dodge and Burn** to add some streaks of shading to it. No need for accuracy here – random streaks is all we need.

17 Use **Filter > Artistic > Plastic Wrap** to add the shine to the tape. There are only three sliders, so experiment with them until you get a good effect.

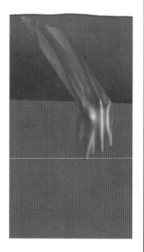

18 Change the mode of this layer to **Hard Light** so we can see through it. Add some red and yellow using **Color Balance**[10]. You may need to darken the whole thing.

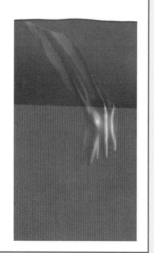

Wrinkles and creases

19 Load up all the box sections as selections, by holding ⌘ Shift ctrl Shift and clicking on their thumbnails in the **Layers Panel**. Make a new **Hard Light** layer, filled with **Hard Light neutral color**. Then inverse the selection and delete everything outside it.

20 Use **Dodge and Burn**[12] to paint wrinkles onto the box. Work slowly at a low pressure, building up the wrinkles as you go.

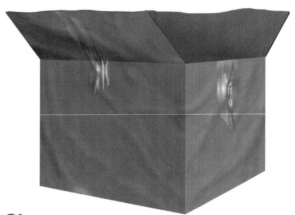

21 Choose a dark brown and paint stains on the **Hard Light** layer. Because our box will be in shadow, I've exaggerated the effect.

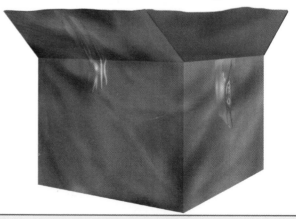

The tearaway

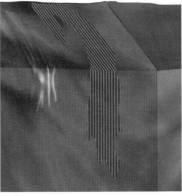

22 Take a piece of the texture created in steps 6–8, and place in perspective on the side of the box. Duplicate to make a perspective section on the flap as well.

23 Make a **Layer Mask** for the tearaway. Make a ragged selection with the **Lasso tool**, and hide the area outside it on the mask.

24 To make the texture blend in better, reduce its opacity. Here, I've reduced it to 50% so we can see some of the underlying texture through it.

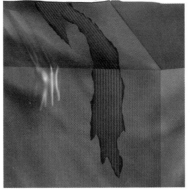

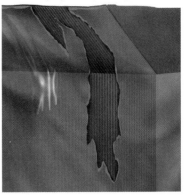

25 Make a new **Hard Light** layer as described in step 19. With a soft-edged **Brush**, paint interior shadows on here in black.

26 Switch to a larger brush and a low opacity, and add some more shading to the interior. Add some shadow beneath the fold.

27 Make a new layer *beneath* the tearaway, and paint edges with a hard-edged brush. Add a little **Noise**, and repeat for the tops of the flaps.

The Fragile stamp

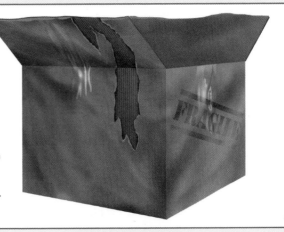

28 Create the stamp on a new layer – this is the **Stencil** font. Use **Layer > Rasterize > Type** to make it into a pixel layer, and then add a couple of lines above and below.

Distort the text to fit the side of the box using **Free Transform**. Then make a **Layer Mask**[7] for the stamp, and run **Filter > Render > Clouds** *on the Layer Mask* to create the faded type effect.

The dress maker's dummy

We don't see these tailoring aids around much any more – and that's largely why they're confined to a forgotten corner of the attic. But they're intriguing objects, and they're a useful way of learning more about drawing and shading.

Shape and shading

1 Draw the outline of the dummy with the **Pen tool**, then make the path into a selection and fill with a mid tone gray.

2 Use **Dodge and Burn** to add shading around the left side, away from the light, and a few highlights on the right.

3 Continue with **Dodge and Burn** to sketch in the shape of the breasts. Subtlety is the key – these are not detailed figures.

4 Use your favorite method to add color to the figure. I used **Curves** to lower the amount of Blue to create this tone.

The fabric texture

5 Make a new layer filled with gray and use **Filter > Texture > Texturizer** to create some basic **Burlap** texture (left).
   Then use **Filter > Distort > Spherize**, set to **Horizontal Only**, to make the texture appear to be wrapped around a cylinder (right).

The mid line

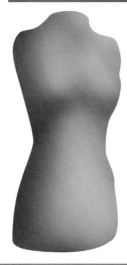

6 Place the texture created in step 5 over the dummy, using the dummy layer as a **Clipping Mask** [7]. Change the mode of the texture layer to **Hard Light** so we can see through it.

7 Draw a path on a new layer that runs down the middle of the dummy, and join the path to the left of the figure. Fill the selection with gray. Use **Layer Styles** to add an **Inner Bevel** to the shape.

8 Change the mode to **Hard Light**, and use the dummy layer as a **Clipping Mask** so we only see the bevel where the two overlap.

The armhole covers

9 Draw an ellipse on a new layer, making sure it fits within the arm area. The ellipse should be slightly smaller than the arm, so we can see some texture to the left of it.

10 Copy a piece of wood texture on top of the ellipse, using the ellipse as a **Clipping Mask** [7] so we only see the wood where the two overlap.

11 Use the **Dodge and Burn tools** to add shading: dark shadows at the bottom and on the left, and a bright section in the upper right. This is a disk, not a ball, so only add strong shading to the edge of the ellipse.

Finishing off

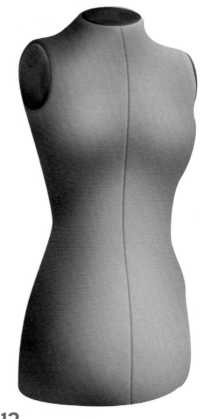

12 Copy the armhole cover to the neck, rotating it 90° so it fits in place, and add a second copy behind the figure for the other arm. Add a little more shading to the figure, if required.

The chipboard panel

To prevent small items from falling beneath the rafters and possibly damaging the ceiling of the room beow, it's common practise to place sheets of chipboard in attics – and they're also handy surfaces to walk on. These are easy to draw, using a rather surprising texture filter.

The chipboard texture

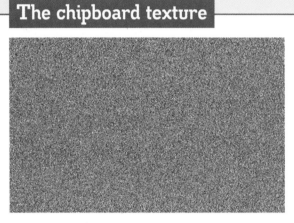

1 Make a large gray rectangle and fill it with gray. Then use **Filter > Noise > Add Noise** to add some **Gaussian Noise**: make sure it's set to monochrome. Choose an amount of around 20.

2 Lock the transparency of the layer, and use **Filter > Blur > Gaussian Blur** to soften the effect slightly. A blur radius of about 2 is generally sufficient.

3 To turn that blurred noise into a piece of convincing chipboard, use **Filter > Distort > Ocean Ripple**. This filter is next to useless when we want to create ocean ripples, but it makes a good chipboard substitute.

   I've used a Ripple Size of 15, and a Ripple Magnitude of 7 – but feel free to vary these settings to experiment with different effects.

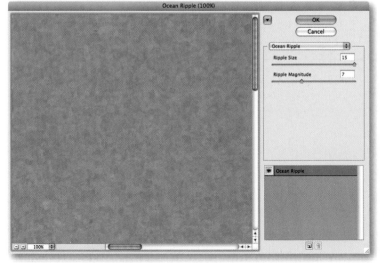

Adding color

4 Use **Color Balance**[10] to add a tan tint. I used **Red +20** and **Yellow -55** to create this tone.

5 We need to darken the chipboard for the dark attic. Use **Curves** to make the whole thing a deeper shade.

Moving into perspective

6 We can now take our chipboard into the attic. Use **Free Transform** to distort it, holding ⌘ ⌥ Shift ctrl alt Shift as you drag a bottom corner handle to distort in perspective.

Bear in mind the vanishing point we determined earlier in the chapter: the sides of the chipboard should point toward this point.

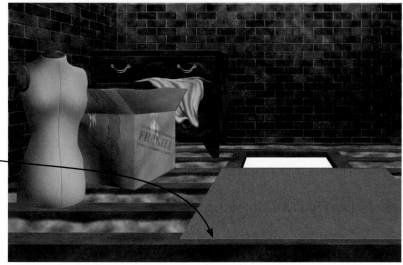

7 Take another horizontal strip of chipboard and place it right at the front, to make the edge facing us.

Darken it (it's away from the light, after all) and then select just the top edge, brightening this up to make it look more realistic.

The guitar

The guitar is one of the most complex objects in this book. But that's not the same as saying it's difficult to draw: broken down into short steps, the guitar is quite achievable by anyone with a reasonable degree of Photoshop skill.

We'll start by drawing the guitar head-on, and then go on to look at how we can create the side-on perspective view.

The guitar body

1 Start by drawing half a guitar shape. The **Pen tool** is really the only way to go about this: if you haven't yet mastered this tool, now's your chance to get its operation pinned down.

2 Duplicate the guitar half and flip horizontally to make the other half. This is the perfect way to create a symmetrical object.

3 Add some wood texture to the guitar base, using the base as a **Clipping Mask.** I've used the earlier of the two wood textures we created on page 24, rather than the deep mahogany grained version.

4 Merge the wood with the base layer, then open the **Layer Style** dialog. This shading is added using an **Inner Shadow**, with a **Choke** about 40% and a **Size** of around 200 pixels. Choose a dark brown color, making sure the mode is set to **Multiply.**

The neck and bridge

5 Draw half the bridge and neck, using the **Pen tool** to get the smoothest results.

6 Copy and clip these halves horizontally. Open the second wood texture (the darker version) and place it on top, using the layer we've just created as a **Clipping Mask**.

7 Select the bridge and cut it to a new layer using ⌘ *Shift* J *ctrl* *Shift* J , then use **Layer Styles** to add a small **Drop Shadow** beneath it.

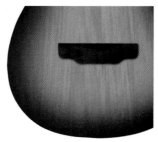

8 Draw half the head of the guitar on a new layer, and duplicate and flip it horizontally to make the other half.

9 Copy the same wood texture on top, using the head as a **Clipping Mask**[7] once again, and darken the whole thing.

10 This is the guitar so far. It's basic, but it's starting to look like a guitar.

The fretboard

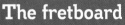

11 Draw a horizontal thin rectangle in brown, on a new layer. Use **Layer Styles** to add a small **Inner Bevel** to it.

12 Duplicate the line several times vertically, making the spaces between the lines progressively smaller with each copy.

13 Place the line assembly onto the guitar neck. You'll then need to use **Free Transform** to make the frets wider at the bottom, lining up with the edge of the neck.

The machine heads

14 Draw a single gray circle on a new layer. Use **Layer Styles** to add a metallic shine to the blob. There are various ways to do this: see pages 16 to 18 for the different options.
 Make five copies, positioned around the headpiece.

15 Duplicate the pieces created in the previous step. Reduce them to about half their diameter, and move the copies so they appear directly above the originals. This is the post the strings will wind around.

The center hole and rings

16 The center hole is just a black circle, placed above the neck layer so it cuts it off. We'll use this circle to build the hole in properly later.

17 Draw a circular selection on a new layer using the **Elliptical Marquee tool**, and use **Edit > Stroke** to apply a thin black stroke to the selection.

18 Make a smaller selection and repeat the stroke process; then repeat a few more times to make a series of concentric decorative rings.

The pegs and bridge

19 To draw the pegs, first make a gray circle on a new layer. Add some shading to it using **Dodge and Burn**, then use **Color Balance** to change it to an ivory color. Finally, draw a small black circle right in the center of the peg.

   Although we're going to make these pegs very small, it's a lot easier to draw them if you work at a much larger size.

20 Arrange six of the pegs on top of the bridge, adding a **Drop Shadow** using **Layer Styles**. This is also a good time to select the outer portions of the bridge itself, adding shadow on one side and a highlight on the other with **Dodge and Burn**.

21 Draw a thin rectangle with rounded ends, add a little shading and color it to make the 'saddle'. Note that this should be placed at a slight angle, rather than absolutely square – that's how it appears in guitars.

Finishing the neck

22 Draw a small gray circle to make the dots on the neck, then duplicate it and place between the frets. The correct arrangement is shown here – the double dots indicate the octave fret. Lock the transparency, and apply the **Clouds** filter before coloring for a pearl effect.

23 Load up the neck as a selection by holding ⌘ *ctrl* and clicking on its thumbnail[6], then add a 3pt stroke on a new layer to make the egde of the neck. Add an **Inner Bevel** using **Layer Styles** to give it some depth.

The string texture

24 The lower guitar strings are wound brass, rather than simple lengths of straight wire. To make this effect, draw two gray circles on a new layer.

25 Use the **Rectangular Marquee** to select the area between the two circles, and fill with the same gray as for the circles themselves.

26 Use **Dodge and Burn** to add shading – light on the top, dark beneath. There's no need to be too fussy here, as this element will be tiny in the finished image.

27 Shrink the string piece down, and duplicate it a number of times to make a stack as shown on the left.

28 Make the whole stack much narrower, then duplicate it to make a single, much longer string. Change the color to brown using **Color Balance**.

Adding the strings

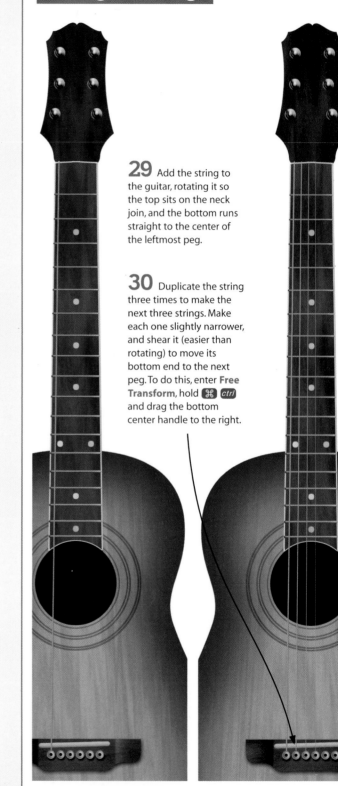

29 Add the string to the guitar, rotating it so the top sits on the neck join, and the bottom runs straight to the center of the leftmost peg.

30 Duplicate the string three times to make the next three strings. Make each one slightly narrower, and shear it (easier than rotating) to move its bottom end to the next peg. To do this, enter **Free Transform**, hold ⌘ *ctrl* and drag the bottom center handle to the right.

Finishing the strings

31 The last two strings are thinner, and are made of single wires, not wound. So draw a straight gray line, using an **Inner Bevel** to give it some roundness, and put in place.

32 We can use **Layer Styles** to add a **Drop Shadow** to the strings, which immediately makes them look more realistic. When we turn the guitar in perspective, though, we'll create our own shadows manually.

33 Take a short section of each of the strings and copy it above the neck join. Then rotate it so that it meets the inner part of the machine heads.

Remember that we created the machine heads in two sections, a back plate and a top peg: move the top peg layer above the strings so they appear between the two machine head elements.

Into perspective

34 While we could have stopped building the guitar at the previous stage, it will look much more realistic if it's viewed from a slight angle, rather than head on.

Select all the elements of the guitar so far, and use **Free Transform** to add perspective. Hold ⌘ *ctrl* as you drag the bottom left handle downward, and an equal and opposite transformation will be produced at the top left corner. This creates a perspective effect as seen here.

Creating the side

35 To make the side, first duplicate the guitar body layer and then move the copy to one side, lifting it up slightly to follow the perspective of the distorted object. Fill the resulting layer with gray, if it isn't gray already.

You'll notice that there are gaps at the top and the bottom, where the duplicate doesn't meet the curve of the base of the guitar.

36 Switch to a small hard-edged **Brush**, using the same gray as the guitar side. Click at the bottom of the side, then hold *Shift* and click at the bottom of the guitar itself. This will draw a straight line between click points, finishing off the bottom of the guitar.

Repeat this process for the top of the side.

The side texture

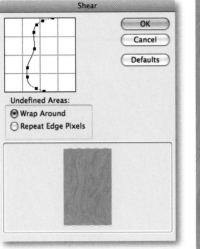

37 Take another copy of the same piece of wood that we used to fill the face of the guitar.

38 Open **Filter > Distort > Shear**, and click and drag on the preview graph to make a shape that looks like the side of the guitar. When we apply this filter, it will distort the wood texture so that it appears to follow the guitar shape.

Shading the side

39 Place the distorted wood above the side, and press ⌘⌥G ctrl Shift G to use the side as a **Clipping Mask**.

40 Darken the side using **Curves**, then use the **Burn tool** to add extra shading at the bottom, beneath the curve of the indent, and at the top.

41 Load up the face as a selection[6], then make a new shaded stroke layer as we did in step 23 of this guitar tutorial.

Realigning the pegs

42 With the guitar now viewed in perspective, we need to move the pegs and the saddle slightly to the right. To give the pegs some thickness, **Select All** and hold ⌥ *alt* as you nudge them to the right with the cursor keys. This will give the illusion of extra depth.

We can do the same with the machine heads, to make them more realistic.

The back of the neck

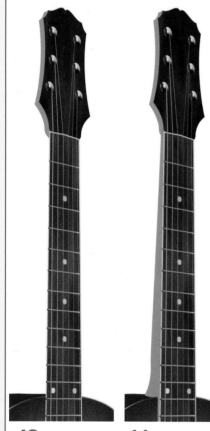

43 Duplicate the head in the same way we did the body in steps 35–36, moving it behind the original and slightly down.

44 Draw the side of the neck on the same layer as the duplicated head, remembering that it gets thicker as it approaches the body. Let it flare out slightly just before it reaches the body.

45 Copy the wood texture onto the neck side, using the drawn side as a **Clipping Mask**[7].

46 Use **Dodge and Burn** to add shading so the side matches the rest of the guitar. Add a shaded stroke to the head, in the same way we added one to the neck in step 23.

47 If you added shadows to the strings earlier, remove them. Duplicate the string layer, fill with black, soften using **Gaussian Blur** and lower the opacity, to make the shadows appear correctly.

Making the sounding hole

48 Cover the black hole we made earlier with a small piece of the usual wood texture.

49 Darken the wood, and make selections to add the suggestion of a structural piece of wood inside.

50 Use the **Burn tool** to add shading, following the shape of the hole so it looks like half of it is in shadow.

51 Select the hole area, and fill with wood on a new layer. Nudge the selection down and left, and delete.

52 Now that we're left with a thin rim – the depth of the piece of wood – we can shade it using the **Burn tool**.

The tuning pegs

53 Draw a simple gray ellipse on a new layer. Add some shading to the edge, and recessed shading in the middle. Flip the layer vertically and horizontally, then duplicate it and flip it back again, reducing it slightly to make an edge; then merge down, and use the metallic **Curves** effect (see page 16) to make it shiny.

The peg posts, right, can be made by copying a piece of the finished tuning peg and stretching it vertically, as well as squeezing it horizontally.

54 Place the tuning pegs in position next to the head: use **Free Transform** to rotate and squeeze a couple so they look like they're at different angles.

Then duplicate the three pegs, move them behind the whole guitar assembly and shrink them very slightly to make the rear versions.

The bicycle wheel

We use the Transform Again command several times in this construction – it's a simple way to replicate an element around a circle, whether it's a hole in the hub, a spoke on the wheel or a bump on the tire. Transform Again is a simple command that can make repetitive transformations a piece of cake.

The inner hub

1 Start with a gray circle on a new layer.

2 Enter **QuickMask**14 (**Q**) and draw a filled circle at the top, then duplicate at the bottom.

3 Enter **Free Transform** and rotate the circles by 20° – type this into the Angle field in the Options Bar.

4 Use ⌘ ⌥ Shift T ctrl alt Shift T to repeat the transformation until the circles run all around. Exit **QuickMask** and delete the selection.

6 Make a small circular selection on a new layer and copy the **Layer Style** to it, then place copies on alternate holes.

5 This is the **Layer Style** we apply to the finished disk. It's a standard **Inner Bevel**, except that we add a **Gloss Contour** – and that's what gives the hub its subtle shine.

7 Draw a new large gray circle, and copy the same **Layer Style** to it. Repeat, then delete an inner circle from all layers.

The spokes and rim

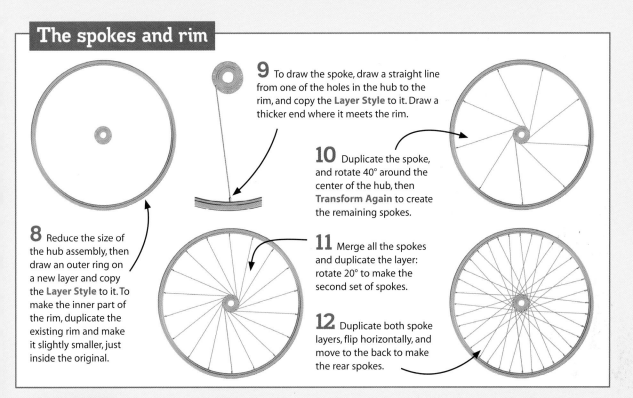

9 To draw the spoke, draw a straight line from one of the holes in the hub to the rim, and copy the **Layer Style** to it. Draw a thicker end where it meets the rim.

10 Duplicate the spoke, and rotate 40° around the center of the hub, then **Transform Again** to create the remaining spokes.

8 Reduce the size of the hub assembly, then draw an outer ring on a new layer and copy the **Layer Style** to it. To make the inner part of the rim, duplicate the existing rim and make it slightly smaller, just inside the original.

11 Merge all the spokes and duplicate the layer: rotate 20° to make the second set of spokes.

12 Duplicate both spoke layers, flip horizontally, and move to the back to make the rear spokes.

The tire

14 Make the first tire bumps on a new layer: a simple circle and rounded rectangle is all that's needed. Select the bumps, and rotate around the center of the hub by 5°; then duplicate all the way around the edge of the tire.

13 To make the tire, start with a thick black circle – make a circular selection and stroke by around 20pt (depending on the type of bike).

15 Merge the bumps with the tire, and use **Layer Styles** to apply an **Inner Bevel** that adds shine and a 3D effect.

16 Make a couple of smaller black rings within the tire area, applying the same **Inner Bevel** as used on the outside of the tire.

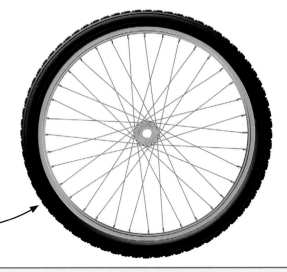

The bowling ball

There are two tricks to drawing this ball. One is to use the Difference Clouds filter to create the initial mottled texture; the second is to use Bevel and Emboss on a Hard Light layer to create the scratches on the surface. Without these scratches, the ball would look far too new and shiny – at least, too new to be consigned to the attic.

The basic texture

1 Make a square selection, choose light gray and dark gray as the foreground and background colors, and run **Filter > Render > Clouds**.

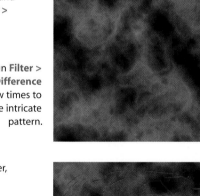

2 Now run **Filter > Render > Difference Clouds** [21] a few times to make this more intricate pattern.

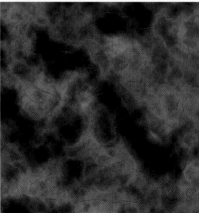

3 Make a new layer, and set its mode to **Hard Light**. Using a small hard-edged **Brush**, paint on here in mid gray. Use the **Layer Style** dialog to add an **Inner Bevel**, and this will make the lines we draw look like scratches on the surface.

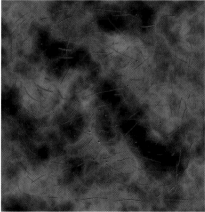

4 Add some pits to the scratches layer by using a hard-edged **Brush** and dabbing small, circular dots onto the surface.

Roundness and holes

5 Make a circular selection as large as you can within the texture, and choose **Filter > Distort > Spherize** at 100%. Then inverse the selection and delete the area outside the circle.

6 Use **Dodge and Burn** to add shading to the ball, with a highlight top right and deep shadow bottom left.

7 To make the holes, begin with a black circle on a new layer. Use the **Layer Style** dialog to add an **Inner Bevel**, but tweak the settings so that both the shadow and the highlight are set to **Screen** mode – after all, there's no point adding a shadow to black. Change the **Shadow** color to a mid gray to apply a visible bevel all around the interior of the hole.

8 Move the hole to one side, and duplicate it. Make the copy smaller, and squeeze and rotate it to make the smaller hole; then copy it again to make the third hole.

9 Select all the holes, **Contract** the selection by a couple of pixels, and fill with gray on a new layer.

10 Load the gray layer as a selection, and move the selection down and then delete it. Shade the remaining gray area.

11 Use **Curves** or **Hue/Saturation** to color the bowling ball according to your preference.

The tennis racquet

There's a surprising amount of detail in a tennis racquet. At least, in the old fashioned wooden variety, rather than the textureless carbon fiber models that are now replacing them. And since this is an old attic, we want the old tennis racquet in here.

The racquet shape

1 Begin by drawing an ellipse on a new layer. The color doesn't matter – we'll be using this as the base for our wood texture.

2 Draw half the handle, using the **Pen tool**. Fill with the same gray on a new layer.

3 Flip a copy of the handle horizontally, and align them both so that the top of the handle blends smoothly into the ellipse of the racquet head.

4 Select and load a smaller ellipse from the center of the head, and delete. The easiest way to do this is to load the head as a selection, enter **QuickMask**[14], and then use Free Transform to shrink it. Finally, merge all the layers.

Completing the frame

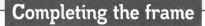

5 Open our standard wood texture, and use the outline we drew in steps 1–4 as a **Clipping Mask**[7].

6 Add a new layer at the top of the handle, and fill with white; add a red stripe at the bottom, or whatever decoration you prefer.

7 Duplicate the original racquet shape and move it to the top of the layer stack. Use **Layer Styles** to add an **Inner Bevel**, and change the mode of the layer to **Hard Light**; adjust its color to a mid gray so the layer itself is invisible, but the bevel effect shows through.

8 Make an elliptical selection slightly smaller than the outside of the head, and use **Edit > Stroke** to apply a 2-pixel brown stroke to it. Repeat this procedure with a slightly smaller elliptical selection.

9 Repeat the stroked ellipse process a couple more times, using a slightly lighter brown to stroke it with. This gives the effect of wood that has been steamed and bent into shape around the edge of the head.

10 On a new layer, draw a round-cornered rectangle and fill with red; apply an **Inner Bevel** using **Layer Styles**. Duplicate this layer and reduce it vertically to make a narrow strip, and then merge the two. Duplicate the result around the head to make the straps that hold the head together.

The handle

11 Make a new layer larger than the handle, and use **Filter > Render > Clouds** to add basic texture.

12 Add a brown color to the texture using your favorite coloring technique.

13 Use the handle as a **Clipping Mask**[7] for the new texture layer. Make a diagonal selection, and use the **Dodge tool** to brighten the top side, and the **Burn tool** to darken the lower side. Then move the selection down and repeat the process until the whole handle is shaded.

16 To make the holes, begin with a gray circle on a new layer. Shade it to look as if it has been lit from the top left, with a shadow cast inside it.

14 Make selections of the top and bottom strip, and use the **Burn tool** to darken these up.

15 Select both sides of the handle with the **Lasso tool**, and **Feather** the selection[4] to soften it. Use **Dodge and Burn** to brighten one side and darken the other.

17 Shrink the hole down and duplicate it to make a row, then duplicate the whole row several times. Move it over the handle, using that layer as a **Clipping Mask**; then reduce the opacity to around 20%.

Adding the strings

18 Draw a horizontal gray line on a new layer. Use the **Burn tool** to darken the bottom edge, then use **Color Balance** to color it pale brown.

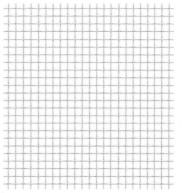

19 Duplicate the line three times, rotating two copies to make a double cross. Erase the top strings where they pass below the lower ones, then use the **Burn tool** to add a little shading to all strings at the cross points.

20 Merge all the strings together, reduce their size if necessary and duplicate to make an array large enough to cover the head of the racquet.

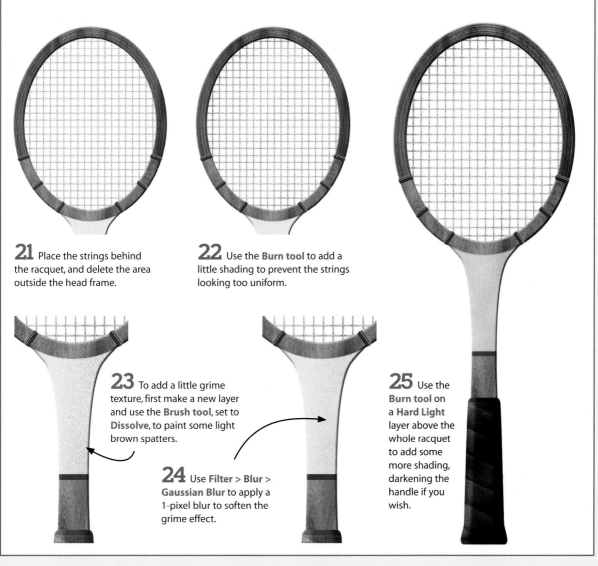

21 Place the strings behind the racquet, and delete the area outside the head frame.

22 Use the **Burn tool** to add a little shading to prevent the strings looking too uniform.

23 To add a little grime texture, first make a new layer and use the **Brush tool**, set to **Dissolve**, to paint some light brown spatters.

24 Use **Filter > Blur > Gaussian Blur** to apply a 1-pixel blur to soften the grime effect.

25 Use the **Burn tool** on a **Hard Light** layer above the whole racquet to add some more shading, darkening the handle if you wish.

The rail station sign

Although it looks impressive, the station sign is easy to create using the Lighting Effects filter, which we've looked at in detail earlier in the book.

The added effect we've added here is some rust, which makes the pristine sign look pleasingly old and battered. Just right for pride of place in our attic.

The basic artwork

1 Start by drawing a gray round-cornered rectangle on a new layer. Delete four holes, one from each corner.

2 Add your choice of lettering to fit the sign. The inner border is made by first drawing a rectangular selection, and then using the **Elliptical Marquee tool** to remove rounded corners from it (this is most easily done in **QuickMask**). Add a stroke to the resulting selection to make the border complete.

3 Add a little noise to the base layer using **Filter > Noise > Gaussian Noise**. We don't need much: around 5% is adequate.

4 Merge all the sign layers together, and use **Filter > Blur > Gaussian Blur** to soften the whole thing, including the lettering. It's the blur that will give the lettering and border their bevel in the next step: a blur of between 1 and 2 pixels is sufficient.

Rendering the sign

5 Copy the merged layer and paste it into a new **Channel**. Use the **Lighting Effects** filter to create the effect – see page 90.

6 Press ⌘⌥6 ctrl alt 6 to load the gray area as a selection from the new channel, then use **Curves**[8] to add red to it.

7 Inverse the selection, and use **Curves** to brighten it up, giving the lettering the impression of having been painted.

Adding the rust

8 Return to the channel created in step 5, and add around 20% **Gaussian Noise** to it. I've also rendered some **Clouds**[20] in here for extra texture.

9 Make a new layer, and run the **Lighting Effects** filter again to create a dense, highly textured version of the sign. Use **Color Balance** to add some red and yellow tint to it, and the **Brightness/ Contrast** adjustment to darken the whole thing.

10 Paint out most of the new rust layer on a **Layer Mask**[7], so it only shows through in small sections.

The bird cage

The cage looks like a much more complex object than it really is. The key to drawing this is to recognise that it's made of a simple wire hoop that's then distorted to make all the rest of the wires.

The chrome technique is one we've used before – it really is the easiest way to make a gleaming metal effect.

The bars and base

 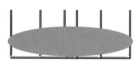

1 Make a circular selection and then add a rectangle at the bottom. Add a stroke to make the basic wire.

2 Apply a metallic **Inner Bevel** using **Layer Styles** – see page 18 for details on how this is done.

3 Duplicate the layer and make it narrower, then apply the same stroke again – otherwise the bars will be too thin.

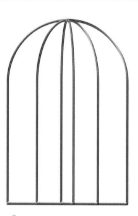

4 Keep duplicating and squeezing, applying the stroke each time, to make more sets of bars.

5 To make the base, start with a gray ellipse; then hold 🔲 *alt* as you nudge it downward to 'extrude' the shape to make a squat cylinder.

6 Select the top of the cylinder, and make an inner stroke on a new layer. This forms the upper edge of the base.

7 Use **Dodge and Burn** to add vertical bands of light and shade to give the base a metallic feel.

8 Delete the initial ellipse, then copy the front and flip vertically to make the back half – move it behind the bars. Add another ellipse, again behind the bars, and darken it to make the base of the cage.

Finishing the bars

9 Add a few more sets of bars using the same process we used in steps 3 and 4.

10 Draw an ellipse and stroke it, and copy the bars' **Layer Style** to it; duplicate the hoop higher up the cage.

11 Cut the two hoops into top and bottom halves, and move the upper half behind the rest of the bars so they appear behind the cage.

12 Add a ring at the top, copying the same **Layer Style** to it. Add some more color and shading to the base to darken it.

Adding the sawdust

13 Paint the sawdust on a new layer, using the **Brush tool** set to **Dissolve** mode.

14 Choose a lighter color to paint some texture into the sawdust, then add some more at a darker color.

15 Use **Filter** > **Blur** > **Gaussian Blur** to soften the sawdust effect, and delete any stray flakes from around the edge.

16 Use **Dodge and Burn** to add a little shading to vary the sawdust texture.

Final steps

17 Add some scratches using a **Hard Light** layer with an **Inner Bevel** – see page 81. Finally, paint a little color onto the cage itself to make it less shiny.

The candlestick

This shiny object is drawn without using any of our standard metal techniques – and that's because the shape of it lends itself so well to hand shading.

The trick to getting this right lies in duplicating the initial shaded shape, and modifying it so that it forms a shiny region that matches the shape of the original.

The shape and basic shading

1 Start by drawing half a candlestick on a new layer. The **Pen tool** is really the only way to do this effectively, although if you really can't get on with it you could always use a series of elliptical selections.

2 Duplicate the candlestick half and flip it horizontally, merging the two layers to create a symmetrical shape.

3 Load up the candlestick area by holding ⌘ *ctrl* and clicking on its thumbnail [6]. Nudge the selected area to the right, then **Feather** it by about 3 pixels to create a soft-edged selection.

4 Use the **Burn tool** to darken the left side of the selection, which leaves the left side of the candlestick untouched – adding the first suggestion of a shine in that area.

The bars and base

5 Move the selection over to the left, then use the **Burn tool** once more to darken the other side.

6 Load up the selection in the same way as step 3, except this time use **Select > Transform Selection** to squeeze it horizontally. Use the **Dodge tool** to add highlights to the center.

7 Duplicate the candlestick layer, and use **Filter > Artistic > Plastic Wrap** to add a few highlights.

8 Duplicate the new layer and change its mode to **Hard Light** to strengthen the whole effect, making it much shinier.

9 Make a series of elliptical selections with the **Elliptical Marquee tool** [4], touching the hard corners of the edge of the candlestick, and use the **Dodge and Burn tools** to add a little shading above and below these 'creases'.

10 Finally, use **Color Balance** to add some red and yellow to turn that candlestick from silver to gold.

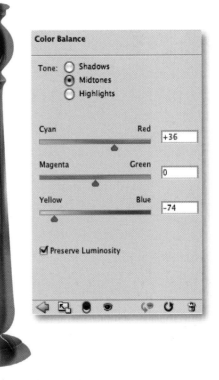

The records

It's the shine on the surface of the records that really brings them to life, making an otherwise flat, dull black surface look glossy and highly lit.

There are several ways to achieve this shine: the method we use, which employs the Polar Co-ordinates filter, is the quickest – and yet it produces spectacular results.

I don't recommend you stack real records like this!

Shape and texture

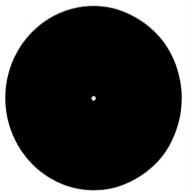

1 Begin by drawing a black circle on a new layer. To remove the center hole, load up the record as a selection, enter **QuickMask**, and use **Free Transform** to scale it down (hold ⌥ *alt* to scale toward the center), and then delete the middle hole.

2 Use the **Layer Style** dialog to apply an **Inner Bevel**. Choose an N-shaped curve in the **Gloss Contour** section to make the shiny edge, shown here in close-up.

3 Make a selection slightly smaller than the record, and make a new layer from it. Use **Filter > Noise > Gaussian Noise** to add the basic noise texture.

4 Use **Filter > Blur > Radial Blur** and set the method to **Spin**. Set the amount to maximum 100% to spin the noise into grooves.

Adding gloss and the label

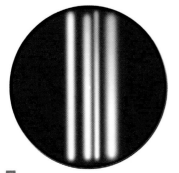

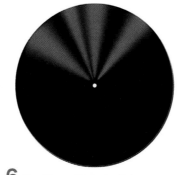

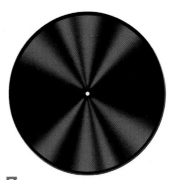

5 On a new layer, paint some vertical white stripes with a soft-edged **Brush**.

6 Use **Filter > Distort > Polar Co-ordinates**, set to **Rectangular to Polar**, to make the radial effect.

7 Duplicate the shine layer and rotate 180°, then use the texture layer as a **Clipping Mask** [7].

8 Make a new layer, and fill a circular selection with black. Use the underlying layers as a **Clipping Mask** so the hole in the middle is still visisble.

9 Make a circular selection, and use **Edit > Stroke** to apply a 3-pixel stroke; repeat with several selections to make the rings dividing the tracks.

10 Choose dark red and black as the foreground and background colors, make a circular selection, and run **Filter > Render > Clouds** to make the label texture.

11 Use the **Shapes tool** to make a circular path, and the **Type tool** to run text around it.

12 Add the rest of the text as you like, set to 50% opacity.

Stacking up

13 Use **Free Transform** to squeeze the record vertically; add a small **Drop Shadow** using **Layer Styles**.

14 Duplicate the record several times. Only the top label will be visible, so we don't need to make any variations.

The light bulb

We'll draw the light bulb in a new document, so we can see what we're doing. To make it come to life, though, we need to change the mode of the glass section to Hard Light, which means we won't see any change on a white background: when we place it against the dark bricks, we'll be able to see the bulb in all its transparent glory.

Shape and gloss

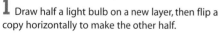

1 Draw half a light bulb on a new layer, then flip a copy horizontally to make the other half.

2 Add some shading around the edge with the **Burn tool**; no need for anything complex at this stage.

3 Use **Filter > Artistic > Plastic Wrap** to add some basic highlights to the bulb.

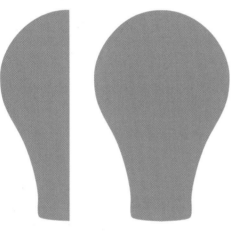

4 Lock the transparency of the bulb layer, and use the **Smudge tool** to smear the highlights around the bulb.

5 Use the **Dodge tool** to add another highlight in the center of the bulb, if necessary. (You may be able to do it all with the **Smudge tool.**)

6 Use **Color Balance**[10] to add a little blue and green.

Inside the bulb

7 On a new layer, draw a torso shape and use **Dodge and Burn** to add a little shading.

8 Run **Filter > Artistic > Plastic Wrap** to make it shiny, then change the layer mode to **Hard Light** so we can see through it.

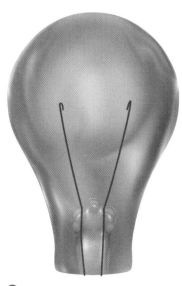

9 Draw the filament holders on a new layer, using the **Pen tool** to draw the shape and then stroking the path with a small, hard-edged **Brush**.

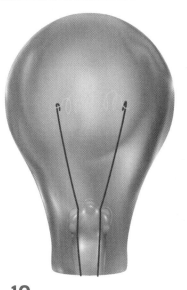

10 Draw the filament on another layer in the same way, and stroke the path with a pale gray. You could also draw this freehand with the **Brush**.

The bulb base

11 Draw an arc on a new layer, beneath the bulb, and fill with pale gray.

12 Select the top half of the shape and shade it using **Dodge and Burn**, then inverse the selection and shade the bottom half.

13 Duplicate the screw layer, and use **Free Transform** to skew it so it takes the form of a screw base.

14 Draw a gray bottom to the screw fitting, below the screw itself.

15 Use **Color Balance** to add a little red and yellow to give the base more of a golden color.

16 Make a new **Curves** adjustment layer, and set its mode to **Luminosity**: then apply a metallic curve shape, as seen on page 16.

The bulb holder

17 Draw a simple ellipse on a new layer, slightly wider than the bulb.

18 Duplicate the ellipse and use the **Rectangular Marquee tool** to join the sides, then fill with gray.

19 Use **Dodge and Burn** to add vertical highlights.

20 Draw a round end cap, and use **Dodge and Burn** once more to paint in some highlights and shadows.

21 Use **Curves** to take out some blue and green, and to darken up the holder.

22 Select thin rims around the top and bottom of the main cylinder, and apply a white **Stroke** at 30% opacity.

Placing the bulb on the page

23 Bring the bulb onto the page, and change the mode of the glass layer from Normal to **Hard Light**[11].

24 To turn the bulb on, use **Curves** to brighten up the glass layer so it looks lit from the inside.

25 Change the color of the filament to white, and use **Layer Styles** to add a small Outer Glow to it.

26 On a new layer behind the bulb, use a large, soft-edged **Brush** to paint a pale glow behind the whole thing.

The crystal ball

We can use a ball we've already drawn as the basis for this intriguing object – no need to draw the same object twice.

Because the key visual element is an inverted and distorted view through it, we need to draw the crystal ball directly onto the page. If we were to move it around, we'd have to redo the refracted view.

Drawing the ball

1 You can draw the basic ball from scratch – or use the ball we created on page 8. Load up the ball as a selection, and then hide it.

2 Use ⌘ Shift C ctrl Shift C to make a **Merged Copy** of the background, then **Paste**. Select it again, then use **Filter > Distort > Spherize** to distort the copy into a ball shape.

3 Flip the copy vertically – that's how a glass sphere would refract the view seen through it.

4 Make a **Layer Mask** for the refracted copy, and paint around the edges to make it fade away.

5 Move the original shaded ball above the refracted copy, and change its layer mode to **Hard Light**.

6 Draw the base as an ellipse, then draw in the sides. Use **Dodge and Burn** to add some dark shading.

The ice skates

These are fairly complex objects to draw, because they have so many constituent parts. The laces, in particular, can be fiddly, but we'll see how to draw a convincing lace and then dupicate it to make all the rest.

Ice skates come in all colors, of course. We'll draw ours in white, but you can always add an Adjustment Layer to tint yours if you like.

The outer skin

1 Draw the skate outline on a new layer, and fill with mid gray. The **Pen tool** is the best way to draw this.

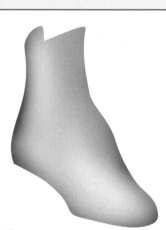

2 Use **Dodge and Burn**[12] to add basic shading around the edge, sketching in shadows in appropriate places.

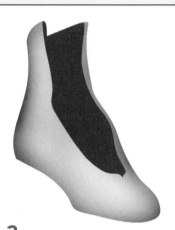

3 Draw the inner part of the skate on a new layer, and fill with gray.

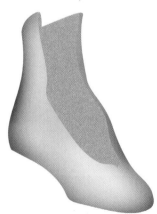

4 Lock the transparency of the inner layer, and apply **Gaussian Noise** followed by **Gaussian Blur**.

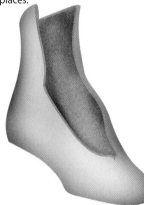

5 Use the **Burn tool** to add some shading to the inside of the interior part of the skate.

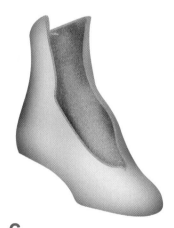

6 Use **Color Balance** to add a pale tan color to the interior.

Drawing the tongue

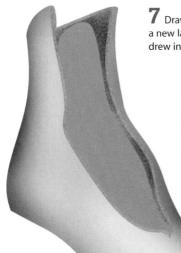

7 Draw the shape of the tongue on a new layer, using the interior layer we drew in step 4 as a **Clipping Mask**.

8 Add some shading using **Dodge and Burn**, and tint the tongue. It should be a little more pink than the interior color we added in step 6.

The base of the boot

9 Draw the sole on a new layer, behind the main body of the skate.

10 Use **Dodge and Burn** once more to add shading, including a slight highlight near the front of the boot.

11 Select a line down the middle of the skate body with the **Pen tool**, and use the **Burn tool** to add a little shading on one side to create the seam.

12 Draw the heel on a new layer behind the sole, filled with gray.

13 Select a vertical line up the sole from the point and including the part beneath the boot, and darken with the **Burn tool**.

The skate base

14 Draw the skate base on a new layer, paying attention to the spikes at the front. Shade with **Dodge and Burn**.

15 Select the bottom of the skate and darken to draw the cutting edge.

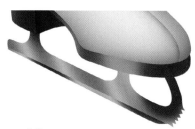

16 Increase the contrast and add some more shading to make it metallic.

17 Select the skate, and hold [⌥] [alt] as you nudge it left and down a few times to extrude it in three dimensions.

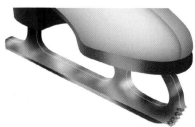

18 Make a new layer from the final copy in step 17, then add a faint **Stroke** to distinguish the side from the inner parts.

19 Lock the transparency of the side layer, and use the **Smudge tool** to clean up any rough edges.

The eyelets

20 Draw the eyelet on a new layer as a disk, then delete the center and shade using **Dodge and Burn**.

21 Add a dark interior to complete the eyelet.

22 Draw the hook on a new layer, adding a little shading on both sides.

23 Move several copies of the eyelets onto the boot, rotating them so they follow the shape of the opening.

24 Place the hooks above the eyelets, copying them to the other side of the skate as well.

25 Add a little shading on the surface of the boot beneath the hooks, to make them stand out.

The laces

26 Draw the first lace on a new layer, in a pale cream color.

27 Use **Filter > Texture > Texturizer** to apply some **Burlap** texture to the lace.

28 Use **Dodge and Burn** to add some shading to make it more rounded.

29 Duplicate the lace several times, rotating each one so that the end appears to come out of one of the eyelets.

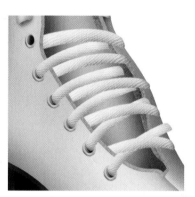

30 Duplicate the laces and move them to the other side, distorting each one so it fits in place; delete the new laces where they disappear behind the boot side.

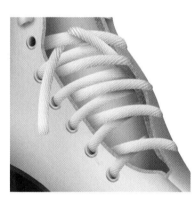

32 Use **Color Balance**[10] to add some color to the boot itself, matching the color added to the tongue.

Make new layers above the tongue and above the boot, and paint shadows on these using a soft-edged **Brush** at low opacity, building it up in small stages.

31 Take another copy of one of the laces and place two versions of it wrapping around the top lace, erasing and shading where necessary.

The copper pipe

This is a straightforward drawing project: both the outside and the inside of the pipe are easy to make. The texture is a simple combination of Noise and Blur – except that this time we'll use Motion Blur to create the horizontal streaks, rather than the more familiar Gaussian Blur.

Once we've created our pipe, we can easily stretch it to any length we choose.

Shape and texture

1 Draw a thin gray ellipse, and copy it to the other end of the pipe. Keep a third copy of this disk, as we'll need to use it later to make the end of the pipe.

2 Use the **Rectangular Marquee** tool to join the two end ellipses, and fill with the same gray.

3 Use the **Dodge and Burn tools** to shade the whole length of the pipe. Hold the **Shift** key as you drag with the tools to draw horizontal shading.

4 Make a new layer, fill it with gray and use **Filter > Noise > Gaussian Noise** to add basic texture.

5 Now use **Filter > Blur > Motion Blur** to streak the noise. Set the angle to 0, and the distance to 200.

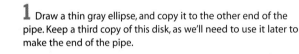

Finishing the pipe

6 Place the blurred Noise layer above the original shaded pipe layer, and change its mode to **Hard Light** so we can see the pipe through it.

7 Move the second copy of the gray disk over the end of the pipe to seal it off.

8 Copy a section of the pipe texture and place over the disk, using the disk layer as a **Clipping Mask** [7]; flip the texture vertically to make the interior of the pipe.

9 Use the **Burn tool** to add some shading at the top of the new texture, so it looks like a shadow.

10 Use **Color Balance** to tint the pipe so it looks like copper: red and a little yellow will do the job well.

11 We can make the pipe as long as we need by selecting one end and moving it away. Then select the rest of the pipe and stretch to fill the gap.

Adding the tape

12 Draw the tape on a new layer. It needs to wrap around the lower pipe, and make a straight line to the top of the upper pipe.

13 Apply a little shading (but not much) with **Dodge and Burn**.

14 Use **Filter > Artistic > Plastic Wrap** to add gloss and shine to the tape we've drawn.

15 Change the mode of the tape layer to **Hard Light** [11].

16 Use **Color Balance** to add a little yellow and a touch of red to the tape.

The picture frame

The broken glass of the frame adds an extra dimension to the image, reflecting the view of the attic back at us. Reflecting the candlestick and cage is easy; if we wanted to include the skates, we'd have to draw them again from the other side.

Making the frame

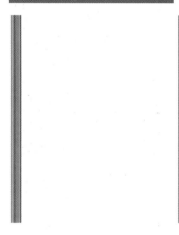

1 Draw a gray rectangle. Then select two vertical strips within it and shade using **Dodge and Burn**; duplicate the side, flip the copy horizontally and move to the other side of the frame.

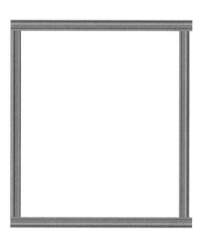

2 Take two further copies of the frame edge and rotate them 90°, in different directions, to make the top and bottom of the frame.

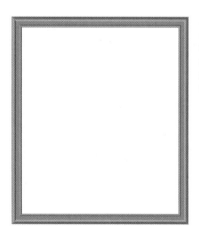

3 Make a **Layer Mask** for the top and bottom sections, and paint out the corners with a hard-edged **Brush** to create perfect mitered corners.

4 Merge all the layers of the frame together. Take a copy of the wood we made on page 24 and place it on top of the frame assembly, setting its layer mode to **Hard Light** so we can see the frame beneath it.

Creating the reflection

5 Place the frame on the page. I've darkened it considerably so it blends in better with the attic surroundings.

6 Make a new layer behind the frame, and fill with mid gray. Use **Dodge and Burn** to add some shadows, and a diagonal streak of light through it.

7 Take copies of the candlestick and cage objects, and place above the glass layer, using it as a **Clipping Mask**[7]. Because the frame is at an angle, we need to rotate the reflections to double that angle.

8 Select the glass, candlestick and cage layers, and choose **New Group from Layers** from the pop-up menu in the **Layers Panel**. Reduce the opacity of the whole group to around 20%.

9 Make a **Layer Mask** for the reflection group, and select a jagged hole on the mask. Fill with black, and this area will hide all the reflected objects.

10 Load up the mask as a selection, and fill with white on a new layer above the group. Then select again and nudge the selection a couple of pixels to the side, and delete: this makes the thickness of the glass.

11 Finish by drawing the string with the **Pen tool**. Choose a small hard-edged **Brush**, and change its mode to **Dissolve**: press *Enter* to stroke the path with the brush to create a ragged effect. Add an **Inner Bevel** using the **Layer Styles** dialog to make the string look a little rounded.

Finishing off: adding the shadows

Shadows make all the difference between a convincing illustration and one that just looks like a random assortment of objects. A lot of shading has been added to this scene.

Shadows can be made on objects by painting them with a soft-edged Brush on a new layer, using the layer beneath as a Clipping Mask.

Alternatively, load the underlying layer as a selection, and make a new Hard Light layer filled with mid gray; then inverse the selection and delete the outside, leaving just a Hard Light layer that exactly matches the layer to which shadows will be applied. Painting on this layer with the Burn tool will create convincing, editable shadows.

Two additional copies of the picture frame – this time without glass reflections – are placed at an angle on the wall, as if hanging from an unseen hook.

Shadows added to the tennis racquets stop them from looking too new and shiny.

The crystal ball is duplicated and placed against the wall, set to **Multiply** mode, to make its shadow.

The shadow of the neck of the guitar is placed twice – once using the dummy as a **Clipping Mask**, and again on the wall behind it.

The shadow of the guitar is distorted when it runs off the dummy and onto the ground plane.

Deep shadows are painted in black on a new layer above the whole composition, adding shading far away from the light source.

The shadow of the bowling ball uses the guitar as a **Clipping Mask**.

It's important to remember to add shadows beneath objects – such as under the chest of drawers and the box.

The shadow of the station sign is placed above it, since the light source is below the sign.

The bicycle wheel layers are duplicated and merged, and then filled with black and offset slightly to create the wheel's shadow.

The shadow of the picture frame is placed to the right, away from the light source.

The interior of the hole is filled with a piece of the wallpaper created on page 32, brightened and set to a very low opacity.

The candlestick shadow is painted directly onto the ground to the right of it, pointing away from the light.

To make the glow through the hole, make a selection the same shape of the hole. Fill it with mid gray, and change the layer mode to **Hard Light**. The layer will be invisible. But when we add an **Outer Glow** to it using **Layer Styles**, only the glow will be visible. The front edge of the glow is painted out on a **Layer Mask**.

The pipe layers are duplicated and merged into a single layer, which is then filled with black and blurred to make the pipe shadows.

Shadows are painted on the ice skates on a new layer, using the skates as **Clipping Masks**; further shadows are painted beneath the skates on the board.

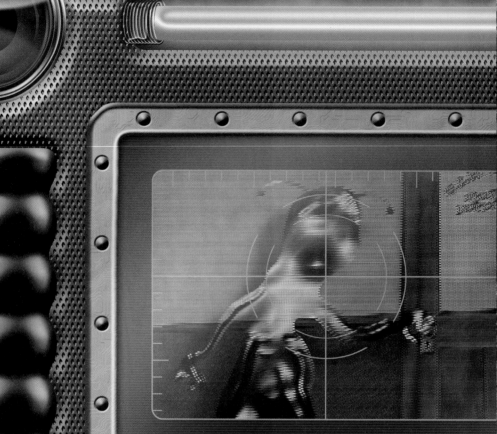

OPTEC ONE
ONLINE
[330, 4022]
INIT STATUS: LIVE
PREP
REALLOC 6, 35A
[334, 4077]
SCANNING..........
.......DETECT MODE
[398, 5126]
REALIGN MODE
[502, 6133.7]

DIFFERENTIAL
CALIBRATING
...001
...002
...005
...103
...159
STEP 1 ACTIVE
REALIGN.....
ALIGN MODE ON
[409, 3391]
INVERSE ACTIVE

DOOR ALARM ACTI
ALERT MODE ALPH
[309, 2991]
[348, 9022]
RESET..........
ACTIVE
INTEGRATING SQU
DEEP HYPERDRIV
[608, 7933]
ALL MODE CHECK
GO GREEN
ACTIVE

Future tech: the scanning machine

In the 1930s, the future was going to be made of bakelite. By the 1960s it was going to be white. By the 1970s, it was looking decidedly silver.

Each generation creates its own vision of futuristic technology, based – naturally – on the technology of the time, interpolated forwards by years or centuries.

Our vision of the future is one that's seen in video games, science fiction movies and comics today. It's a rugged, grungy, tactile future where weaponry is far removed from the ice black, slick iPhone interface we currently use.

Mapping out the shapes

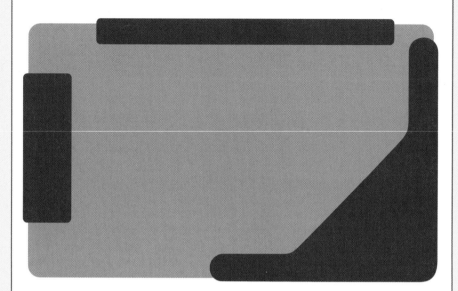

1 With an object as complex as this one, it's a good idea to sketch out the basic shapes at the outset. The easiest way to do this is to use the **Shapes tool**, creating a new **Shape** layer with each operation. The advantage of this approach is that we can modify the shapes as we go along; as they're defined by vector paths, we can tweak them as much as we like without loss of quality.

Using the **Shapes tool** effectively does require a good knowledge of the **Pen tool**, although a lot can be accomplished with just the round-cornered rectangle shape tool.

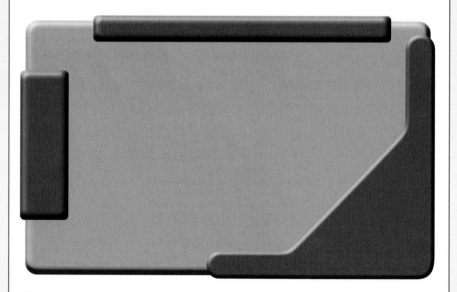

2 Adding a large **Inner Bevel**[17] to all the shapes, using the **Layer Styles** dialog, is a big help in making the shapes look more three-dimensional. Although we'll redraw some of these shapes, the basic background and the stretched triangle on the side will form the basis of the finished artwork.

The side grip

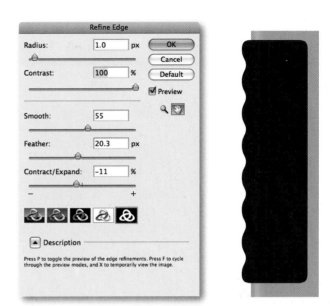

1 Start by drawing a series of horizontal bars on a new layer, then draw a vertical rectangle on the same layer that unites them all.

2 Load up the shape as a selection[6], then open the **Refine Edge** dialog. Set the contrast to 100%, and raise the **Smooth** and **Feather** values. This will soften the selection edges considerably. When the shape is right, click OK and fill the shape with color on a new layer.

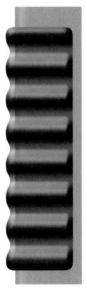

3 Use **Layer Styles** to add a wide **Inner Bevel**[17], to give the grip some thickness.

4 Make a **Layer Mask**[7] for the layer, and use a soft-edged **Brush** to paint horizontal stripes through the shape. This hides the bevel as well as the layer, making these ridges.

5 Disable the **Layer Mask** by holding *Shift* and clicking on its thumbnail in the **Layers Panel**: this reveals the layer itself fully, but still hides the bevel effect.

6 Paint a vertical stripe on the right of the mask to fade the bevel away on this side. Because the **Layer Mask** is disabled, only the bevel is affected.

7 Copy a section of the left side of the grip, and move it to the right, flipping it horizontally. This now appears the other side of the vertical stripe in the mask.

The segmented control ring

The multi-button ring is created as a simple circle, divided into eight and given a three-dimensional effect using a Pillow Emboss technique.

I'm not entirely sure as to the purpose of the glowing green ball inside the ring. Perhaps it's a planetary scan – or it might just be a scroll ball. You decide.

The segments of the ring

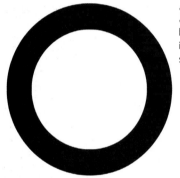

1 Start by drawing a ring on a new layer. The easiest way to do this is to draw a circle, then delete a smaller circle from inside it.

2 Make a **Layer Mask**[7] for the ring, and make a thin vertical selection; fill this selection with black to hide a vertical stripe down the center of the ring.

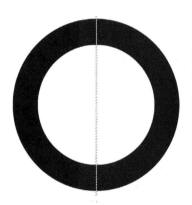

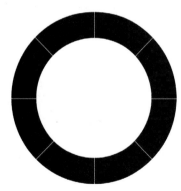

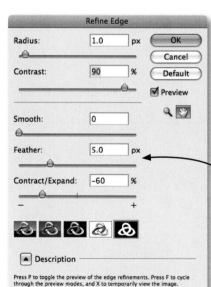

3 Rotate a copy of the stripe 90° to make a horizontal line, then rotate by 45° in both directions to make the further divisors.

The ring should now be divided into eight equal segments.

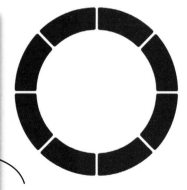

4 Load up the ring as a selection, and use the **Refine Edge** dialog with a large **Feather** amount to soften the edges. Use the **Contract/Expand** slider to make the selection slightly smaller, then make a new ring layer using the selection.

Finishing the ring

5 Use **Layer Styles** to add an embossing effect to the ring. Use a **Pillow Emboss** for a recessed effect.

6 Add a dark blue color to the ring. I've also added a texture to the background shape, using the **Clouds** filter.

7 Select one segment of the ring, and make a new layer from it; add an **Inner Glow** using **Layer Styles**, set to **Center**.

8 Draw an inner circle, filled with gray. This will form the basis of the glowing ball inside the ring.

9 Use **Dodge and Burn** to add some basic shading to the circle. It shouldn't be too even, so use a lot of short strokes.

10 Use **Filter > Artistic > Plastic Wrap** to add shine to the circle, making a glossy spherical effect.

11 Add an outer ring, using **Layer Styles** to add an **Inner Bevel** to give it a three-dimensional appearance.

12 Color the ball using **Hue/Saturation**. I've chosen a luminous green color for this ball.

13 Draw an ellipse at the top of the ring, and **Feather**[4] the edges; paint the bottom white with a soft-edged **Brush**.

The microphone and angled buttons

A second set of buttons surrounds the segmented ring we drew previously, following the shape of the corner and cut away from the ring buttons. The microphone is rounded to make it appear raised within its recessed casing.

The microphone

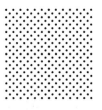

1 Draw an array of dots on a new layer. The easiest way to do this is to draw one dot, select it, then hold ⌥ Shift / alt Shift as you nudge copies of it to the side.

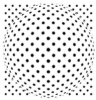

2 Make a circular selection within the dots, and use **Filter > Distort > Spherize** to make them into a ball. Inverse the selection, and delete the outer dots.

3 Separate the spherized dots into two halves, the distance between the halves making the full width of the microphone.

4 Select two vertical columns of dots, and duplicate horizontally to fill the space between the two ends. This makes a 3D lozenge of dots.

5 Fill the dots with white, and place on a black background that matches the shape of the lozenge – but keep the dots as a separate layer.

6 Use **Layer Styles** to add an **Inner Shadow** to the dot layer: make the distance very small, as the dots themselves are tiny. Add an outer ring layer, using an **Inner Bevel** to make it shiny – see page 18 for more on this technique.

The angled buttons

1 On a new layer, draw a triangle that matches the angle of the corner piece, and which encloses the segment ring. Move this layer behind the segment ring layers.

2 Delete a circle from the new layer, slightly larger than the ring. Then use the **Refine Edge** technique described earlier in this chapter to round off the edges of the remaining triangle segments.

3 Use **Layer Styles** to add a **Pillow Emboss** to the triangle segments. This type of emboss has an effect both inside and outside the layer, producing a recessed appearance.

4 Make a **Layer Mask**[7] for the buttons layer, and delete a horizontal rectangular shape from the left set of buttons, and a vertical rectangle from the right set. This divides the buttons into four.

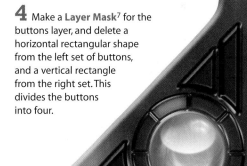

5 Make two new selections on the **Layer Mask** to delete vertical and horizontal sections from the larger buttons, dividing each of these into two.

6 Color the buttons, and use **Layer Styles** to add an **Inner Glow** to them. Set the mode to **Center** so just the interior lights up. I've also brightened and colored one of the buttons to make it look selected.

The liquid tube

As this is a piece of fantasy technology, we don't need to be too precise about the exact purpose of most of the controls and features. A bit like buying a computer, really. The tube of bubbling liquid adds interest and color in the vertical segment of the corner piece; and that's reason enough to include it here.

The metal frame

1 Start by drawing a lozenge on a new layer. There are several ways to do this; the easiest is probably to use the **Shapes tool** to draw the initial shape, modifying it as needed to stretch it to the size we want.

2 The simplest way to turn the lozenge into an outline is to select it by holding ⌘ *ctrl* and clicking on its thumbnail in the **Layers Panel**. Make a new layer, then use **Edit > Stroke** to apply a white stroke around the edge.

3 Draw in a series of horizontal bars all the way down. The simplest method is to draw one using the **Rectangular Marquee tool**, and then fill the selection with white; hold ⌥ *alt* as you drag the selection to make multiple copies. You may need to adjust the bottom to make the spacing even.

4 Use the **Refine Edge** technique describe earlier in this chapter to round off the edges. This step helps to create an object that looks like it has been cast in metal, rather than one that has simply been drawn.

5 Make a rectangular selection of the middle section, including all the horizontal bars, and use the **Image Warp** mode of **Free Transform** to apply a **Bulge** distortion. Change the mode from the default horizontal to vertical, and drag the handle to stretch the bars.

The liquid interior

6 Apply an **Inner Bevel** with a **Gloss Contour** to make the bars look shiny – see the description on page 18 for how this is done.

7 Make a new layer behind the bars – you can use the original lozenge shape if you haven't deleted it – and fill with blue as the basis for the liquid.

8 Use **Dodge and Burn** to add shading around the edges, giving a rounded effect to the tube.

9 Use the **Dodge tool** to add a vertical highlight, which emphasizes the glassy feel of the tube.

10 Add a **Layer Mask**, and make an elliptical selection near the top. Fill the selection with mid gray to partly hide the liquid layer, producing an air effect above.

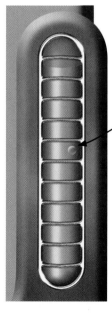
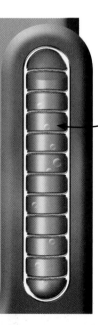

11 To draw the first bubble, make a circular selection on a new layer, and use a small soft-edged **Brush** to paint a little white on the top left and a little less white on the bottom right.

12 Duplicate the bubble, reduce it in size and drag copies around the interior of the tube.

13 Reduce the bubble again, and drag several copies to fill the tube with bubbles. They'll look more convincing if a few of them overlap.

The camera

We're going to place our camera bulging out of the top left corner of the device. This adds visual interest to the overall shape, breaking the rectangular nature of the object.

The lens looks complex, but it's an easy object to draw: it's the light flares, added at the end, that give it the glassy appearance that makes it read as a lens.

The outer ring

1 Begin with a gray ring on a new layer. The simplest way to draw this is to make a circular selection and then add a **Stroke** to it.

2 Use the **Layer Style** dialog to add an **Inner Bevel**. The **Ring** shape in the **Gloss Contour** section creates the shine.

To make the shape more detailed, switch to the **Contour** pane and add an **Inverted Cone** contour.

3 Duplicate the ring layer and make it smaller, and move it behind the original. This time, we'll add a sawtooth **Gloss Contour** shape for the ridges.

Gloss Contour:

The camera lens

4 Make a gray circle on a new layer behind the rings, and use **Dodge and Burn** to add shadows and a highlight to it.

5 Duplicate the layer, make it slightly smaller, and rotate 180° to make the first of the inset sections of the lens.

6 Duplicate the layer once more, make it smaller again, and rotate it 180° again to make the second of the inset sections.

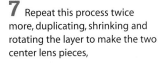

7 Repeat this process twice more, duplicating, shrinking and rotating the layer to make the two center lens pieces,

The light flare

8 Make an elliptical selection behind the outer ring, but in front of the inner ring. **Feather** the selection[4], and use a soft **Brush** to paint the bottom edge white.

9 Repeat this process at the bottom of the lens, this time painting in green: set the mode of this new layer to **Hard Light** so we can see the lens through it.

10 Duplicate the green layer and rotate it, reducing its size at the same time. Color this version magenta to finish the lens construction.

The base plate

With the main elements in place, we can turn to that flat base and make it match the shape of the added objects. The first thing I've done here is to darken it so it recedes more into the background: this makes the brighter elements, such as the camera and the corner piece, stand out better.

Bevel and texture

1 We already have an **Inner Bevel** on this base plate. To make it fit the placed objects, load up their selections by holding ⌘ Shift ctrl Shift and clicking on their thumbnails in the **Layers Panel**. Make a **Layer Mask** for the base plate, and fill this selection with black: as the selection is hidden, the bevel will mold itself to the cutout shapes.

2 Draw two diamonds (see page 75 for an easy method) and offset them. Make a rectangular selection around them, and choose **Edit > Define Pattern**.

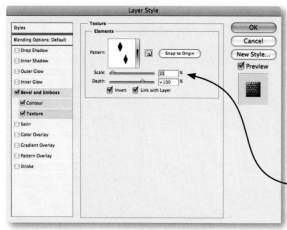

3 Open the **Layer Style** dialog for the base plate, and check the **Texture** box in the **Bevel and Emboss** section. Choose the diamonds as the texture, and scale until it looks right. I've also added a blue tint to the base plate.

The holes array

4 Make a grid of dots, on a new layer, the width of the bottom part of the base plate. Offset every other row as seen here.

5 Duplicate the dots layer, and make a selection that just encloses the dots. Use **Filter > Distort > Spherize**, set to **Horizontal Only**, to create this distortion.

6 Use **Free Transform** to squeeze the distorted dots so that the dots in the middle appear round – they will have been stretched in the previous operation.

7 All we want from the **Spherize** step is the lower half of the dots: join this to the original dots to make the bottom look as if it curves away around a rounded edge.

8 Take a section of the rounded dots and move it to the left, so that the dots now appear to curve away on the left as well. You'll need to erase a few stray dots for a convincing rounding effect.

9 Fill the dots with a mid gray, and use **Layer Styles** to add a very small **Inner Shadow** to them. This turns the dots into an array of holes.

The aluminum base

10 Load the original base plate as a selection[6], then hold `⌘` `⌥` `Shift` `ctrl` `alt` `Shift` as you select a rectangle as high as your array of dots to limit the selection to the bottom area. Make a new layer, and fill with gray.

11 Use the **Dodge tool** to paint diagonal stripes on the gray to make a shiny effect. Using a very small brush size, drag the tool again along the top, with the `Shift` key held down, to brighten the top edge.

12 Duplicate the layer, and add some **Gaussian Noise**; then use **Filter > Blur > Motion Blur**[23] to add horizontal streaks to simulate brushed aluminum. Set the mode of this new layer to **Hard Light** so we can see the shading beneath.

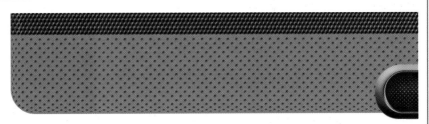

The light bar

It may be a scanner, it may be a signal light – or it may be a bar of radioactive material. Whatever you decide, the glowing beam forms a strong area of interest at the top of the device, complete with fizzing output.

This is a simple object to draw. The fizzy smoke coming off it is created using the Clouds filter – again, it isn't nearly as complicated as it looks.

The bar shape

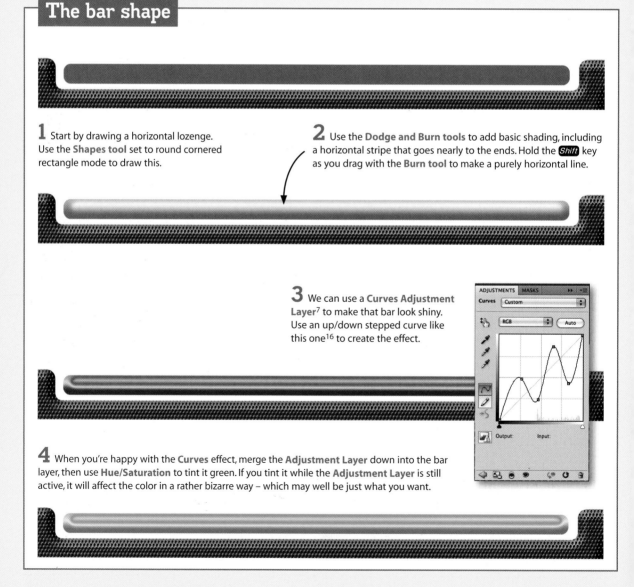

1 Start by drawing a horizontal lozenge. Use the **Shapes tool** set to round cornered rectangle mode to draw this.

2 Use the **Dodge and Burn tools** to add basic shading, including a horizontal stripe that goes nearly to the ends. Hold the *Shift* key as you drag with the **Burn tool** to make a purely horizontal line.

3 We can use a **Curves Adjustment Layer**[7] to make that bar look shiny. Use an up/down stepped curve like this one[16] to create the effect.

4 When you're happy with the **Curves** effect, merge the **Adjustment Layer** down into the bar layer, then use **Hue/Saturation** to tint it green. If you tint it while the **Adjustment Layer** is still active, it will affect the color in a rather bizarre way – which may well be just what you want.

Finishing the bar

5 To hold the bar to the device, we need some clips. Draw a stroked ellipse on a new layer, and use **Layer Styles** to add a shiny **Inner Bevel** to it.

6 Hold `ctrl` and click the Layer Style in the **Layers Panel** to bring up the pop-up menu. Then choose **Create Layers** to turn the effect into a regular layer; merge it with the ellipse.

7 Make several offset copies of the layer, merge them together and set the mode to **Hard Light**. Copy the assembly to both ends of the light bar.

8 When we add a black background to the image, we can see that the light holders are too transparent.

9 Create a new layer behind them, and paint some gray into it to make a more solid backing for the holders.

10 The glow on the light is easily added using the **Outer Glow** section of **Layer Styles**: choose a green that matches the lamp.

11 To make the gas, make a new layer and set the foreground/background colors to green and black. Then use **Filter > Render > Clouds**.

12 Paint out the edges of the cloud layer in black to make them more prominent in the center, to complere the effect.

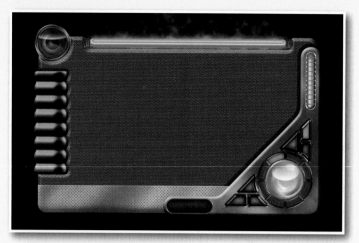

The screen

It's a known fact that in science fiction, some technologies advance while others regress. When *Star Trek* crew members beam down to the planet's surface, the Bridge crew can hear them but can't see what they see: video phones have yet to reach deep space.

So it is that screens in sci-fi movies are grainy, monochromatic, and prone to the sort of disruption we haven't seen on terrestrial televisions in decades.

The screen frame

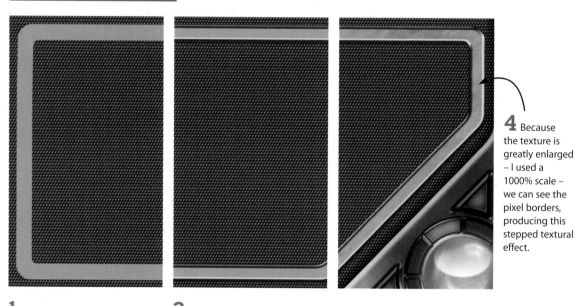

4 Because the texture is greatly enlarged – I used a 1000% scale – we can see the pixel borders, producing this stepped textural effect.

1 The basic frame is drawn in gray, on a new layer. There are several ways to make this. The simplest is probably to draw the outer shape with the **Pen tool**, and then **Stroke** it with the Stroke setting set to **Inside** to create the whole frame. We can't perform a **Center** stroke, as with a stroke this wide the outer stroke would be segmented and jagged.

2 Use **Layer Styles** to apply a glossy **Inner Bevel**, as we have done several times in this chapter.

3 Make a large **Cloud** texture in a new document, and define it as a **Pattern**. Now, when we switch to the **Texture** section of the **Bevel and Emboss** dialog we can apply that texture, embossed onto the surface of the border.

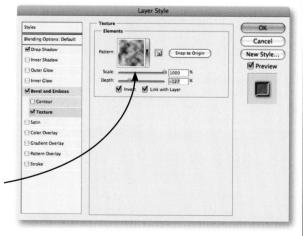

The frame and alien screen

5 The rivets are simply a row of circles on a new layer, with a **Pillow Emboss** to recess them.

6 Duplicate the rivets, and apply an **Inner Bevel** to the copy to make them dome-shaped.

7 For the screen background, make a new layer inside the frame area and fill it with black.

8 The texture is a regular pattern of horizontal lines, colored green and placed on the black background at a low opacity.

9 The background to the on-screen display is the hallway we drew in Chapter 2. I've used **Free Transform** to distort this so it appears as if we're looking up at the scene from below – it's a more menacing view than straight on, and makes the alien look more eerie.

10 The alien is drawn in gray, and shaded with **Dodge and Burn**.

11 Use **Filter > Artistic > Plastic Wrap** to make the alien glossy. Increase the contrast, and duplicate for the shadow.

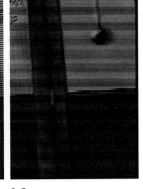

12 Merge the on-screen layers together, and color green.

13 Place a grid of horizontal lines over the top, and merge with the on-screen layer.

14 Duplicate the layer, and set the mode to **Difference**: offset it a few pixels to make the break-up pattern.

The frames and ticks

16 To make the frames, make selections and stroke them with green.

17 The ticks are drawn as horizontal lines, in the same way as the ruler on page 80.

15 The circles are made by drawing a circular selection and then applying a thin stroke to it. A square is then selected that intersects with this circle, and then deleted to leave the arcs at the top, bottom and sides.

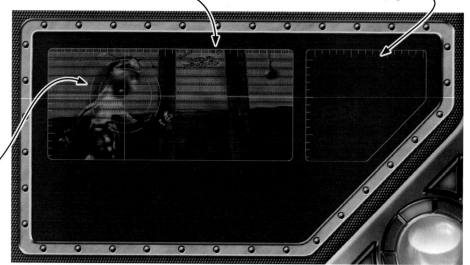

The bar shape

18 The radar is a gradient, applied to a new layer. To start, choose **Gradient Overlay** in the **Layer Style** dialog.

19 Set the mode of the gradient to **Angle**, and click inside the gradient preview to open the **Gradient Editor**. This gradient has the same green at both ends.

20 The **Clouds** filter creates the texture; the blip dots are just painted on in white, with an **Outer Glow**.

The top set of markers sets the transparency within the gradient

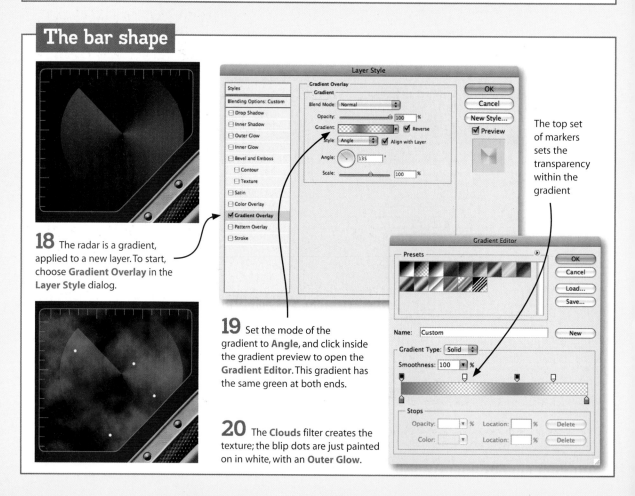

Adding the text

21 The text is set in several columns – but in Photoshop we have to do this one column at a time. It's pure techno babble, of course, but it still takes a while to compose.

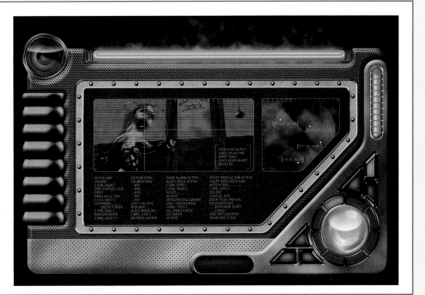

Finishing off

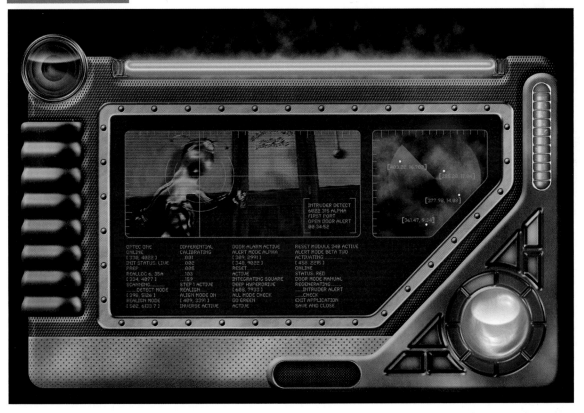

22 To complete the image, load up all the key layers as a selection[6] – the base, the camera, the projecting corner, the grip – then make a new layer above them all, set to **Hard Light** mode. Paint on here in shades of brown, red and blue, at a low opacity, to add the effect of stains and shading – and to add interest to the piece.

CHAPTER 8
The Great Outdoors

Painting the sky

Natural textures and objects are among the hardest to create in Photoshop. But taken in short steps, what seems like an impossible job can easily be broken down into a series of short, manageable tasks.

We'll start with drawing clouds. This is one of the few texture occasions where we won't begin with the Clouds filter – as we've seen, this otherwise useful filter is awful at creating realistic clouds.

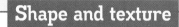

Shape and texture

1 Begin with a new layer, filled with black. This is necessary, since the filters we'll use next only work with a background.

Sketch out the cloud shape using a soft-edged brush, at a fairly low opacity, and build up each cloud in small stages. Remember that clouds appear smaller as they approach the horizon, so place the larger ones at the top.

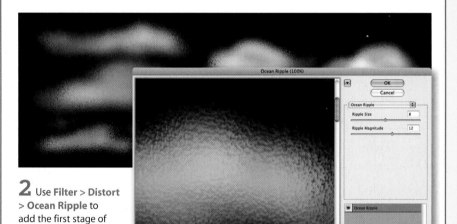

2 Use **Filter > Distort > Ocean Ripple** to add the first stage of roughness to the clouds.

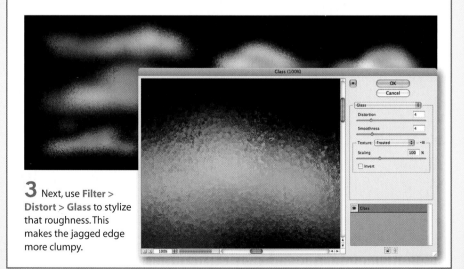

3 Next, use **Filter > Distort > Glass** to stylize that roughness. This makes the jagged edge more clumpy.

Shading and streaking

4 We now need to lift the clouds off that black background. The easiest way to do this is to **Select All**, then enter **QuickMask** mode[14] by pressing **Q**. Then **Paste**, and the cloud assembly will be pasted into QuickMask so it can be used as a selection. The black may be selected, depending on how you have QuickMask set up, so you may need to invert the image in order for the clouds to be selected.

5 Leave **QuickMask** by pressing **Q** again, and make a new layer, filling the selected area with pale gray. This is also a good time to place the sky behind: a simple graduation using the **Gradient tool**, using two shades of blue as the foreground and background colors, should do this.

6 Use the **Dodge and Burn tools** to add shading to the clouds: bright at the top, darker shadows beneath. It's worth using a low pressure and building up the effect slowly.

7 For more realism, use the **Smudge tool** to streak out parts of the cloud horizontally. Vary the size of the tool to get more variety in the cloud shape.

The grass brush

To paint our grass, we need to define a custom brush. We'll end up defining several brushes in the course of this chapter, so we'll look at this first one in some detail to show how it's assembled.

The initial shape

1 Draw a single blade of grass on a new layer. If it's drawn in gray, as it is here, the brush will be translucent – and that's the effect we want. To create a solid brush, paint in black. I used the **Pen tool** to draw the shape for this brush, but you could also draw it freehand.

When the shape is finished, select it with the **Marquee tool** and choose **Edit > Define Brush Preset**.

Starting the modification

2 As it stands, our brush is not yet fit for purpose. Open the **Brushes** panel, and choose the newly created brush (it will usually be the last one in the list). Click the **Shape Dynamics** box and move to that pane: set the **Size Jitter** to 100%. When we paint with this brush, we get the size variation as shown below.

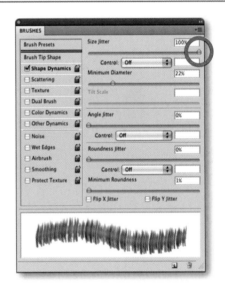

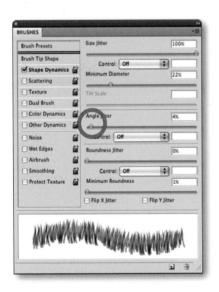

3 All those blades of grass are too regular – they're all pointing straight up. So raise the **Angle Jitter** value slightly: I've chosen a low figure of just 4%, since we don't want too much variation in angle.

Now, when we paint with the brush we get varying angles as seen below, which is starting to look far more convincing.

Finishing the brush

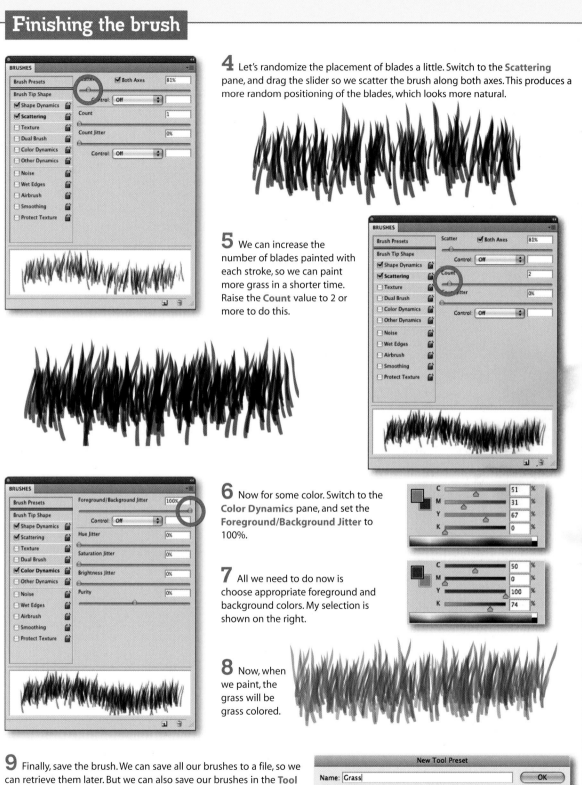

4 Let's randomize the placement of blades a little. Switch to the **Scattering** pane, and drag the slider so we scatter the brush along both axes. This produces a more random positioning of the blades, which looks more natural.

5 We can increase the number of blades painted with each stroke, so we can paint more grass in a shorter time. Raise the **Count** value to 2 or more to do this.

6 Now for some color. Switch to the **Color Dynamics** pane, and set the **Foreground/Background Jitter** to 100%.

7 All we need to do now is choose appropriate foreground and background colors. My selection is shown on the right.

8 Now, when we paint, the grass will be grass colored.

9 Finally, save the brush. We can save all our brushes to a file, so we can retrieve them later. But we can also save our brushes in the **Tool Preset** panel: this allows us to save their color, as well.

Painting the grass

With our grass brush created, we can now go on to paint grass around our image.

We'll need to paint it in several layers to get the perspective effect right – after all, it should be large in the foreground and small in the background.

Map out the grass area

1 It helps to sketch out the area we're going to paint with grass. Use a green that matches the grass color, so no white gaps are seen through the blades. I've also drawn in a gray area where the water will appear, in a new layer.

Painting the grass in place

2 Using the grass brush we made on the previous pages, paint a large portion of foreground grass on a new layer.

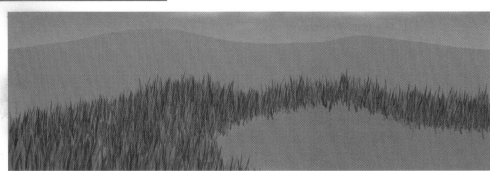

3 Reduce the size of the brush (you don't need to redefine it, just press **[** to make it smaller) and paint more grass on a new layer behind the first one.

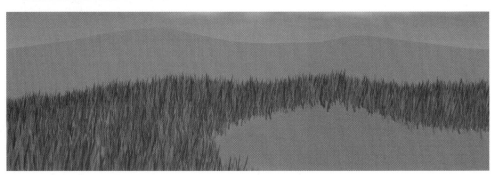

4 Keep adding new layers, varying the brush size as you do so. I've darkened and brightened some for variation. Add a larger layer of grass right at the bottom.

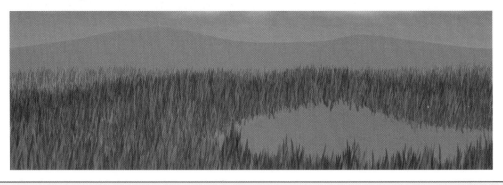

The distant hills

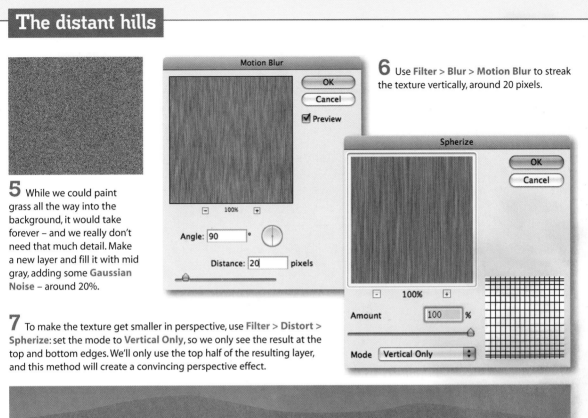

5 While we could paint grass all the way into the background, it would take forever – and we really don't need that much detail. Make a new layer and fill it with mid gray, adding some **Gaussian Noise** – around 20%.

6 Use **Filter > Blur > Motion Blur** to streak the texture vertically, around 20 pixels.

7 To make the texture get smaller in perspective, use **Filter > Distort > Spherize**: set the mode to **Vertical Only**, so we only see the result at the top and bottom edges. We'll only use the top half of the resulting layer, and this method will create a convincing perspective effect.

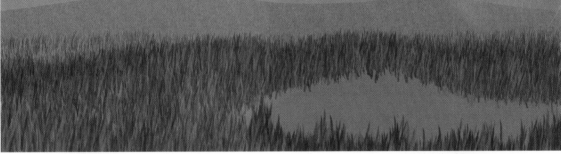

8 Colorize the filtered noise layer to turn it green, and move it to use the hills layer as a **Clipping Mask**[7].

9 I've added a smaller version of the texture to make some more faraway hills, adding a little brightness as well.

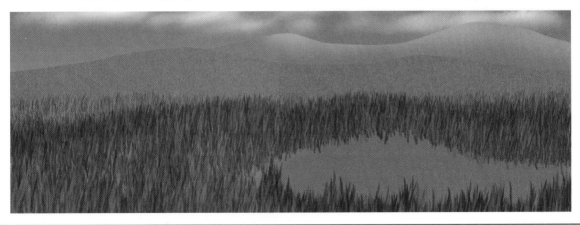

The tree trunk

Most of our tree will be covered with leaves. But we'll still be able to see the trunk, and the bottoms of the branches, so we need to make a bark texture to cover them in.

Trees come in a huge range of textures: this one's suitable for the kind of old oak we might find in our rustic surroundings.

The bark texture

1 Make a rectangular selection and choose two browns as foreground and background colors: run the **Clouds** filter.

2 Use **Filter > Render > Fibers** to create the beginnings of the bark texture. Try out different **Variance** and **Strength** settings.

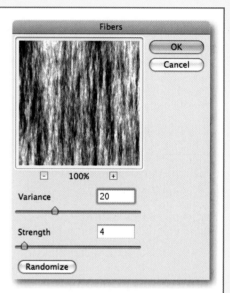

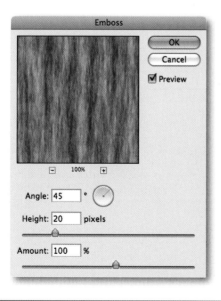

3 Duplicate the layer, and run **Filter > Stylize > Emboss** to give a more three-dimensional appearance to the texture.

4 Change the mode of the Embossed layer to **Hard Light**, and merge it down into the original texture layer.

Placing the bark on the tree

5 Sketch out the shape of the tree on a new layer. The color doesn't matter – we're only concerned with getting the shape as we want it at this stage.

6 Make a selection inside the bark created on the opposite page, and feather the edges to soften them. Place the copied selection over the bottom of the drawn tree.

7 Switch to the **Move tool**, and hold ⌥ *alt* as you drag copies of the bark, rotating and moving them until the whole tree is covered with the texture. The feathered edges should help mask any joins.

8 Make sure all the bark is merged together into a single layer, and choose **Filter** > **Liquify**.

Use the **Forward Warp tool** within the **Liquify** filter to smear and twist the bark so it follows the shape of the branches. Use the other tools to twist some areas into knots.

Squeeze the texture at the sides of the main trunk, so it appears to wrap around the trunk in perspective. This will make the three-dimensional effect more convincing.

9 The **Liquify** filter, used in the previous step, is the key to making the texture look like part of the tree.

Once this step is complete, make sure the texture is directly above the tree outline layer, and use it as a **Clipping Mask**[7] so the bark only shows up where it overlaps the outline. You may want to roughen up the outline a little for a more naturalistic appearance.

The leaves on the tree

With the trunk completed, we can place the tree into the illustration. Placing it behind the front section of grass makes it look more naturally sited in the scene, as the grass grows up in front of it.

The leaves are created in the same way as we made the custom brush for the blades of grass, earlier in this chapter.

The leaf

1 We start by drawing a single leaf as an outline, in dark gray so it will be partially translucent.

2 Select half the leaf and darken it, to make a fold down the middle.

3 Use a small brush to paint veins on the leaf.

4 When the leaf is finished, use the technique on page 200 to make a custom brush.
Set the **Angle Jitter** to 100% for the new brush, and adjust the **Scatter** amount so the leaves overlap – we don't want any stray leaves.

The first layer of leaves

5 Choose appropriate green colors for the foreground and background, and paint the first set of leaves in the tree using the leaf brush you've just created.

6 Use the **Burn tool** to paint some shadows into the leaves, so they make the next layer – added on top – stand out from the background.

Finishing the tree

7 Make a new layer, and paint some more leaves on this, inside the existing leaf area. Adding a **Drop Shadow** using **Layer Styles** helps give the tree a three dimensional appearance, as it makes the front set of leaves stand out from the back set.

8 Continue to add more leaves as needed, filling in the spaces. Use the **Burn tool** to add shading, giving the illusion of depth to the tree and making it less uniform in appearance.

9 Reduce the brush down to a very small size, and choose slightly more muted tones of green as the foreground and background colors. At this smaller size, the leaf brush can be used to paint convincing ivy growing up the trunk of the tree: paint it in continuous lines, reaching up from ground level.

This brush makes such good ivy that we'll go on to use it throughout the illustration, adding it to our house and fence to give everything an overgrown look.

Finally, put all the layers of the tree into a new **Layer Group**, then duplicate the group. Use ⌘ E ctrl E to merge its contents, and fill the resulting single layer with black. Use **Free Transform** to shear and compress it to make the ground shadow, then lower the opacity and use **Gaussian Blur** to soften the edges.

The house: stone texture

We built a brick wall earlier in this book, but rough stone is a different matter. Here's a technique I've worked out that produces lumpy, jagged stonework with the minimal amount of effort.

The only laborious part is drawing the brick outlines – and there's no shortcut for that.

The brickwork

1 Start by drawing the shape of the front wall, on a new layer. Don't make the edges too regular – this is supposed to be a broken, rustic cottage.

2 Draw in the stones on a new layer. Draw large, square blocks at either end of the wall, and either side of the door, for structural purposes. Leave spaces above the door and window for the lintels.

The mask texture

3 This is the texture we'll use for making the stone mask. Begin with a simple **Clouds**[20] filter on a new layer.

4 We need a smaller texture, so scale the layer down and duplicate it, flipping alternate pieces horizontally so they join.

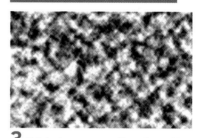

5 Use **Brightness/Contrast**[10] to increase the contrast of the texture, making it much more stark and strong.

Texturing the stone

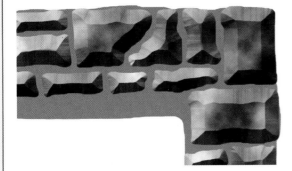

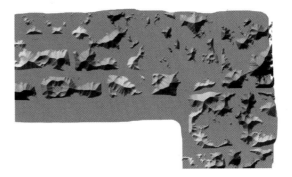

6 Fill the stone layer with gray, and add an **Inner Bevel** using **Layer Styles**. Set the bevel **Technique** to **Chisel Hard**, to make the crisp edge seen here.

7 Now select the texture created in steps 3 to 5, and **Copy** it. Make a **Layer Mask**[7] for the stone layer, and paste the copied texture into the mask to make the effect above.

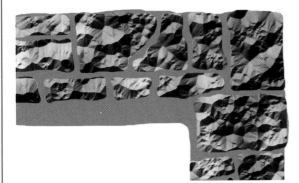

8 Hold *Shift* and click on the Layer Mask's thumbnail in the **Layers Panel**. This disables the mask effect for the layer, but still applies it to the **Layer Effects**: that's what creates the lumpy stone texture.

9 Switch to the original wall, and add a little **Gaussian Noise** followed by a small amount of **Gaussian Blur** to create the basic texture for the cement.

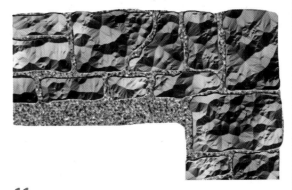

10 Use **Filter > Unsharp Mask** with a radius of around 200% to strengthen the effect of the cement texture. The effect we want is of small stone chippings mixed in with the cement.

11 Load up the stone area as a selection by holding ⌘ *ctrl* and clicking on its thumbnail, then, still on the cement layer, make a new layer from the selection. Use **Layer Styles** to add a **Pillow Emboss**, to make the stone look inset.

Build the house

With the front wall constructed, we can place it into the illustration and add all the elements that will make it look like a real building.

All the other pieces we'll need – the ivy brush, the wood for the door and lintels, the sky reflected in the window – we've already created, either earlier in this chapter or earlier in the book, so it's just a matter of putting it all together.

The house in perspective

1 Use **Free Transform** to distort the front wall so that it lies in perspective within the artwork: hold ⌘ ⌥ *Shift* *ctrl* *alt* *Shift* and drag one of the right corner handles to create the perspective effect.

Pay attention to the position of the horizon, which is just below the hill level: the top and bottom of the house should point toward this line for the perspective to look correct.

2 The stone texture we created on the previous pages now looks too crisp and bright in the context of this image. Use **Brightness/Contrast** to lower the contrast until a more natural appearance is achieved.

To make the house break up at the top – which saves us from having to draw a roof – make a **Layer Mask**[7], and use a hard-edged **Brush** to paint out the stones in a ragged manner.

3 Copy sections of the stonework to the right of the door and window, and flip them horizontally to make the thickness of the walls. Lower the brightness, and use **Free Transform** as necessary to make them appear to sit correctly inside the openings.

Creating the lintels

4 The wooden lintels form the upper part of the door and window openings. We can use a piece of the wood we made on page 24 to fill the space we left.

5 Select the lower portion of both lintels, using the **Lasso tool** – hold ⎇ **alt** to trace a straight line. Darken the selection to make the underside.

6 For a stronger effect, duplicate the lintel layer, desaturate (⌘ U ctrl U) and change the layer mode to **Hard Light** to create a deeper tone.

Building the interior

7 Duplicate the front wall and scale it down to make the back wall; flip a copy horizontally to make the side wall. Darken the lower parts of the new walls, leaving the top bright where the light catches it. Paint out a new area on the **Layer Mask** so it differs from the front.

8 To make the ground inside, make a new layer and fill with mid gray. Use a little **Gaussian Noise** and **Gaussian Blur** for texture, and add some color. For extra realism, make a new layer and paint some grass inside.

9 To make the walls a little dirtier, make a new layer and choose a large, soft brush set to **Dissolve** mode. Paint on the wall in brown at a low opacity, then use **Gaussian Blur** set to a radius of 1 pixel to soften the result.

Making the door

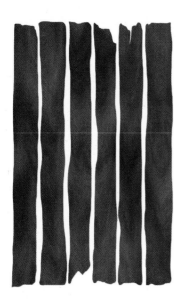

10 Open the wood we made on page 24, and make irregular vertical selections as shown here.

11 Drag the planks into the artwork, and use **Free Transform** to add perspective. Darken to a more muted tone.

12 Duplicate the plank layer, and move it behind the original. Darken it to make the thickness of the planks.

13 The horizontal door pieces are made in the same way as the vertical planks. The top of the bottom plank is brightened, not darkened.

14 Duplicate the whole door assembly, and merge the layers together; desaturate, then change the mode to **Hard Light** to add texture strength.

15 To make the door and the house look more part of the scene, make a new layer in front of them and use the grass brush to add some blades in front.

Adding the ivy

16 On a new layer, use the leaf brush we made on page 206 to paint ivy around the door and on the top of the wall.

17 Adding a **Drop Shadow** using **Layer Styles** adds depth and realism to the ivy. But we don't want the shadow to show on the sky: so add the area outside the house as a **Layer Mask,** then disable the mask using the technique on page 208, steps 7 to 8.

Making the window

18 Draw the window frame on a new layer – make rectangular selections and copy to make the whole frame.

19 Add an **Inner Bevel** using **Layer Styles**; add the wood texture on top for realism.

20 Copy a piece of the sky, and place behind the window frame to make the reflection.

21 Make a **Layer Mask** for the reflection layer, and fill jagged **Lasso** selections with black to make the holes.

22 Fill the holes with white, on a new layer. Then nudge the selection up and to the left a couple of pixels.

23 Delete the new selection from the white layer to leave the glass edge, and reduce the opacity to 50%.

The fence

The fence serves to tie the foreground into the background. As the image stands, the distant hills don't yet feel part of the same illustration as the tree and the house. By placing the see-through fence into the artwork, we create a visual link between the front and back of the image, unifying the whole into a more coherent illustration.

Building the fence

1 We can make the horizontal fence rails in just the same way as we made the door planks: make horizontal but wiggly selections in the wood texture, and distort to fit the space.

2 The vertical fence posts are pieces of the bars rotated by 90°. They can be placed in front of the rails, on their own layers.

3 To make the side of the posts, duplicate the layer and darken the copy. Move it behind the original, and offset it to the left. You may need to erase parts of the top to make it look like a single piece of wood – by default there will be a jagged corner.

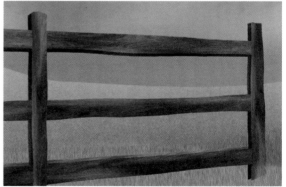

4 We can make the tops and bottoms of the rails in the same way. In order to make them fit the perspective, we need to be able to see the top of the bottom bar, and the bottom of the top one – so squeeze the copy vertically. This time, though, we'll brighten the top of the bottom rail.

Adding grass and ivy

5 We can use the leaf brush we created on page 206 to paint ivy onto the fence. Use a small brush size, and paint it so it climbs up the posts and then drips off the horizontal rails.

6 Adding a **Drop Shadow** using **Layer Styles** makes the ivy stand away from the fence. But there's a problem: we can see the shadow against the sky, as well as against the rail.

7 To fix the problem, load up the fence rails and posts by holding ⌘ *Shift* *ctrl* *Shift* and clicking on each thumbnail in the **Layers Panel**. Then **Inverse** the selection, and fill this area on a **Layer Mask**[7] on the ivy layer.

8 Adding the **Layer Mask** hides the layer, of course, and it also hides the effects. If we disable the mask by holding *Shift* and clicking on its thumbnail, we reveal the layer again but the effects remain hidden.

9 To complete the ivy effect, make a new layer behind all the fence layers, and paint some ivy dripping down here – the other side of the posts and rails.

10 Finally, make a new layer in front of the fence, and use the grass brush we created on page 200 to add some grass in front of the whole lot, blending it into the ground.

The pond

Right in the foreground, the pond is one of the main focal points of the illustration. It looks appealing and even refreshing, but it isn't a difficult object to draw.

There are two distinct stages: adding the reflections from elements already in the image, and then turning those reflections into a convincing rippled surface.

The reflections

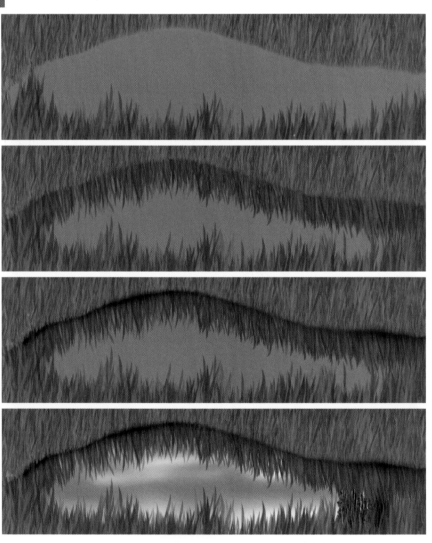

1 We sketched out the pond area earlier on, when we made the hills. We then added grass in front, and the grass stuck down over the pond: now's the time to make a **Layer Mask**[7] for the grass, painting it out to make a soft edge.

2 Duplicate the grass layer above the pond, and flip it vertically. Use the **Image Warp** mode of **Free Transform** to twist the grass so it follows the shape of the pond. You may find it easier to do this in several sections.

3 Paint a new layer, darkening the edge between the grass and its reflection. I've also darkened the reflected grass slightly for a more convincing appearance.

4 Duplicate the cloud layer and flip vertically, placing it behind the reflected grass. Make a copy of all the tree layers, merge them together, and flip them so we can just see the trees behind the reflected grass.

The water texture

5 Place all the reflected elements into a new **Layer Group**, and load the pond area as a selection: use this as a **Layer Mask** for the group. Reduce the opacity of the group to around 50%.

6 Duplicate the **Group**, and **Merge** its contents into a single layer. Then use **Filter > Distort > Glass** to add some basic rippling to the new composite layer.

7 Duplicate the original pond layer, and bring it above the reflections. Run the **Clouds** filter, followed by the **Glass** filter, to make the rippled surface.

8 Change the mode of the new texture layer to **Hard Light**, so we can see the reflections through it. Then merge the two layers together to make a single pond layer.

9 Make an elliptical selection with the **Elliptical Marquee tool**, and use **Filter > Distort > Zigzag** to make the concentric ripple effect. Experiment with the height and number of ripples until you get a good looking result.

10 Make a couple of additional elliptical selections, and run the **Zigzag** filter again to distort the surface in these new areas. Placing a zigzag over the edge of the tree reflection will produce a strong ripple.

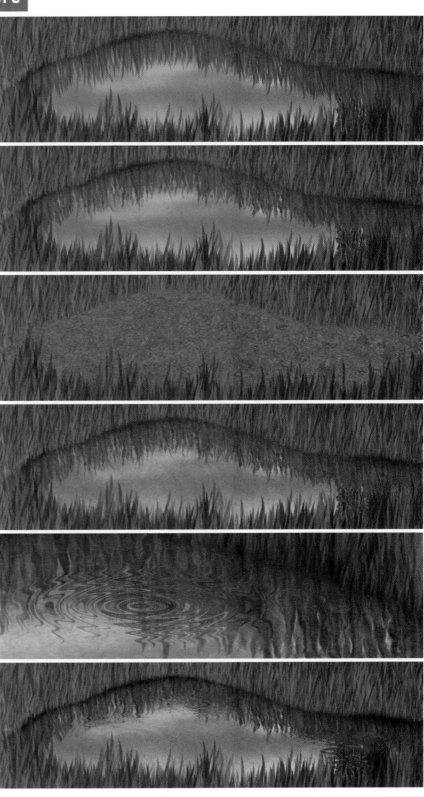

The flowers and hill trees

All that wide expanse of grass looks a little featureless: some tiny spring flowers will help to liven it up, adding interest and making the grass look less regular. And we can make the brow of the hill more appealing by adding a small forest to it.

The distant trees

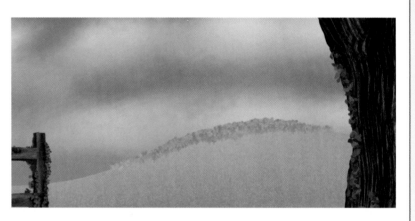

1 We can easily create a new brush for the trees, using the procedure we saw on page 200. This time, a soft-edged tree outline will suit the purpose. Keep the foreground and background colors pale, to emphasize the distance.

The flowers

2 The flower brush is easy to construct: it's just a pair of ellipses, which are then rotated to make the basic flower shape. Make a new brush as described on page 200, and paint small flowers in clumps around the artwork. Use a smaller brush for the more distant flowers.

Finishing off

With all the elements in place, there's not much left to do to complete our illustration. A few final tweaks will make it more convincing and more picturesque – and that, after all, is why we're doing this in the first place.

The final touches

Adding a little perspective to the clouds using **Free Transform** gives added depth.

A new custom sheep brush allows us to paint a flock of distant sheep on the hillside.

Lichen can be painted on the tree with a tiny custom flower brush, then blurred slightly.

Brighter areas painted on the wall make for a dappled sunlight effect.

Brightening the blue sky near the horizon increases the sense of distance.

A few fallen leaves on the pond add interest. Use the existing custom leaf brush, and squeeze the result vertically to create the perspective viewpoint.

Brightening the right side of the tree on a new **Curves Adjustment Layer** adds the sense of sunlight.

CHAPTER 9

Still Life

Still Life

Painters and photographers
have been depicting still
life images for centuries.
The interest comes from
the interplay of texture,
composition and lighting,
giving artists the chance to
demonstrate their skills.

Still life images vary
considerably in content, from
the fruit and dead game
birds favored by the Old
Masters to the dismembered
body parts portrayed by the
contemporary photographer
Joel Peter Witkin.

Whatever the choice of
subject, the themes often
entail death and the passing
of time: our skull and
metronome show both of
these concepts.

Drawing the table

1 Once again, we'll begin with a piece of the wood texture we drew on page 24. Use **Free Transform**[6] to squeeze this into a perspective viewpoint.

2 Use **Curves** to darken the wood, adding some red for a richer tone.

3 Duplicate a piece of the wood and darken it to make the front edge.

4 To make the edge itself, paint a horizontal white line on a new layer.

5 Reduce the opacity of this layer to a very low figure – I've used just 10%. It's barely visible, but it makes a difference: the edge is now well defined.

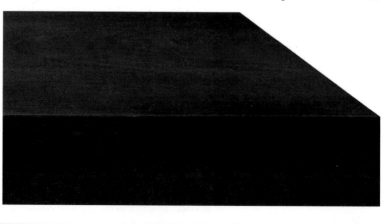

Making the background

1 Use the **Clouds** filter[20] to create the basic texture, using two shades of light and dark brown.

Because the filter creates small, intricate patterns, I've taken a section of the texture and enlarged it to fill the whole background space. The enlargement makes it softer as well.

2 It's not worth obsessing over exactly the right foreground and background colors to use with the **Clouds** filter. It's always possible to adjust the hue and contrast afterwards.

Here, I've darkened the texture up to make a dull mottled wall.

3 Shadows are the key to making this illustration work well. Make a new blank layer behind the table construction, and use a very large, soft brush to paint black around the edges of the image.

The space in the middle is left clear for the candle. Because this is a separate layer, we can always add to it and erase parts of it later if we need to.

The red cloth

Since we're using a lot of hard objects in this construction, we need something soft to balance the image, providing more textural variety.

We looked at how to draw a sheet in the Attic chapter, on page 126; here, we'll use a similar technique to make this piece of rich, dark fabric.

Shape and basic shading

1 Begin by drawing the shape of the cloth. It's best to use the **Pen tool** to draw the outline, although it's also possible to draw this freehand with a hard-edged **Brush**.

2 Use the **Burn tool** to paint shadows around the edge of the whole cloth. This starts to give it a three-dimensional feel.

3 Use the **Dodge and Burn tools** to sketch in the approximate location of the folds and wrinkles. There's no need to be too precise at this stage, as most of the work will be done later; all we're doing is suggesting where the folds will be.

Use the **Dodge tool** first to paint the highlights at the top of the folds, then switch to the **Burn tool** to paint shadows beneath them.

Fine shading and color

4 Lock the **transparency** of the cloth layer, and use the **Smudge tool** to smear the shadows and highlights, to create the initial folds. This is much easier than it looks: choose a soft-edged **Brush**, with a **Pressure** of around 80%.

5 We can smear the dark edge into the cloth as well, which helps us to create the deep shadows beneath large folds. Because we locked the transparency, we don't smudge the edge of the sheet.

6 Use the **Burn tool** once more to strengthen some of the shadows, adding deep shading beneath the folds. Again, there's no need for accuracy at this stage.

7 Continue to smear with the **Smudge tool** until the cloth properly takes shape. It can take a while to build up the texture, but it's an enjoyable and relatively easy process.

8 Finally, use the **Hue/Saturation** adjustment[11] to add a deep red color to the cloth (check the **Colorize** box to begin adding color).

I've also darkened the front edge of the cloth, where it hangs over the table, since this area will receive no direct light and very little reflected light from the candle.

The skull

Organic forms are always harder to draw than manufactured objects, and our skull is no exception. Rather than trying to paint it, though, we'll make full use of the Smudge tool, which – as we saw in the previous exercise – is a great way of creating folds and wrinkles and other natural shapes.

Overleaf, we'll look at adding texture and detail to the skull; we'll begin, however, with the basic shape.

Shape and basic shading

1 Draw the outline of the skull on a new layer. As with any life drawing, it really helps to have a skull – or at least a photograph of one – to base this on.

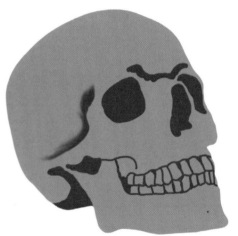

2 Draw in the eyes, teeth and bone shapes *on the same layer*. Add in dark shadows under the back of the skull and inside the nose area.

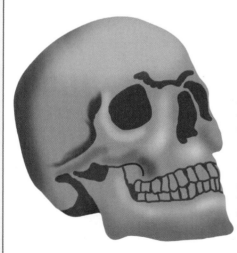

3 Use the **Dodge and Burn tools** to paint in highlights and shadows on the tops and bottoms of the main bones. There's no need for accuracy here, the shading will just form the basis for the **Smudge tool** to work on.

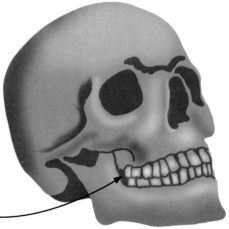

4 Use the **Dodge tool** to paint highlights inside all the teeth – just a dab will do – and around the edge of the nose cavity.

Smudging the shading

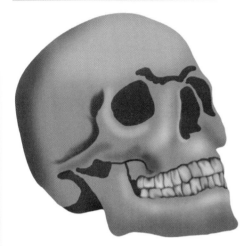

5 Use the **Smudge tool**, with a small brush size, to smear some of the dark area above and below the teeth into the teeth themselves.

6 Continue to smudge the shadows into the skull – above the eyes, inside the nose – smearing with a soft brush tip to soften the hard edges where the shadows blend into the skull.

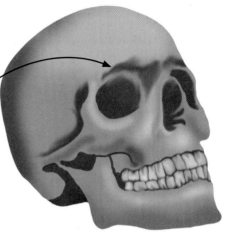

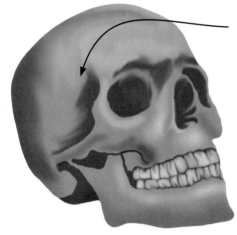

7 Use the **Smudge tool** to smear the dark shadows above the cheek bone into the skull, and to smear the shadow at the left edge into the skull as well.

8 Smear the dark areas on the jaw, and at the base of the skull, so they blend into the rest of the shape.

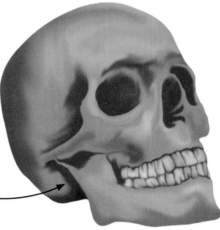

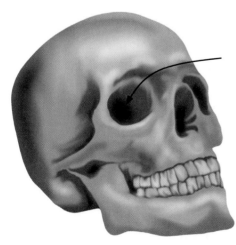

9 Keep smudging and smearing to make all the hard shadows blend in. At this stage, it can help to use the **Burn tool** to darken some of the deepest areas – inside the eyes and nose, beneath the cheekbone, and at the base of the skull.

10 Keep on with the **Smudge tool**, blending in the tops and bottoms of the teeth for realism.

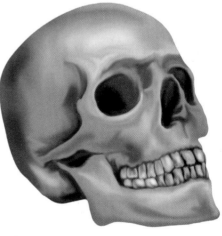

Pits and cracks

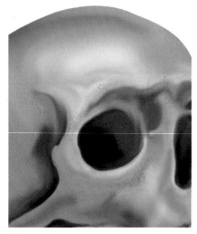
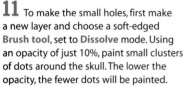
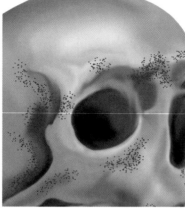
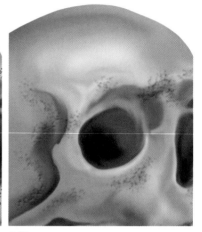

11 To make the small holes, first make a new layer and choose a soft-edged **Brush tool**, set to **Dissolve** mode. Using an opacity of just 10%, paint small clusters of dots around the skull. The lower the opacity, the fewer dots will be painted.

12 To make the dots larger, choose **Edit > Stroke** and add a 1-pixel stroke outside the selection. With no selection made, this will simply make the tiny dots larger.

13 Use **Filter** > **Blur** > **Gaussian Blur** to soften the dots slightly, then add an **Inner Bevel** using **Layer Styles**. This creates the recessed appearance.

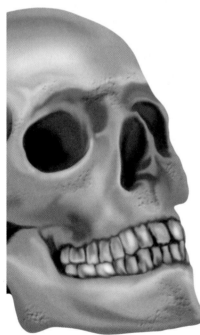
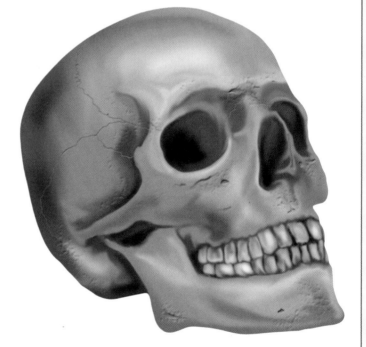

14 If the effect is too harsh, lower the opacity of the layer – or use a soft-edged **Eraser**, at a low opacity, to paint out some of the dots to lower their strength. The effect should be subtle, rather than overpowering.

15 Use a small, hard **Brush** at a low opacity to paint the tiny cracks between the plates that make up the skull, as well as adding a few additional pits and crevices on the jaw and beneath the eye sockets. As you paint, the **Inner Bevel** will make the cracks and pits appear to be recessed into the skull.

Adding texture

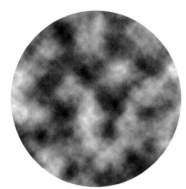

16 To create the bone texture, start with a circular selection on a new layer and user **Filter > Render > Clouds**.

17 Use **Filter > Stylize > Emboss** to turn the cloud effect into a rough, stone-like texture.

18 With the circular area selected, choose **Filter > Distort > Spherize** to create the rounded effect.

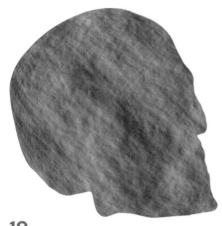

19 Stretch the texture until it covers the whole skull. Then use the skull layer as a **Clipping Mask**[7] so the texture is visible only where it overlaps it.

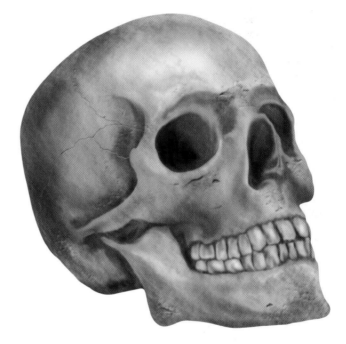

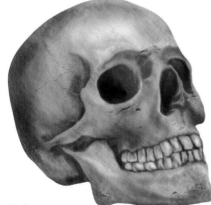

20 Change the mode of the texture layer to **Hard Light** so we can see through it, reducing the opacity of the layer if necessary.

21 Use a **Hue/Saturation Adjustment Layer** to add color to the skull. The settings I used are shown here (with the **Colorize** box checked).

   To make the color less uniform, paint out parts of the mask that comes with the **Adjustment Layer** with a soft-edged brush, on a low opacity: this will hide the coloring effect, allowing a little of the original gray to show through, so making the skull that much more realistic.

Hue:	36
Saturation:	20
Lightness:	0

The old books

Although the book is apparently a complex object, it can be pieced together in a series of small steps – like almost everything else in this book.

As always, we start out by creating the texture, and then drawing the shape of the book in flat gray layers before applying the texture to those layers.

The leather texture

1 Choose two rich brown shades as foreground and background colors, and run **Filter > Render > Clouds** to make the basic texture, as seen below.

2 We need to crisp this texture up. Use **Filter > Sharpen > Unsharp Mask**, with fairly high values – I used a 400% setting, with a radius of 6 pixels.

Building the covers

3 Draw the upper cover of the book on a new layer. It's easiest to do this with the **Pen tool**, as this allows the four corners to be adjusted easily.

4 The right edge is drawn on a new layer, again using the **Pen tool** for preference – although this could be done with a hard-edged **Brush**.

5 Draw the spine on a new layer, darkening it so we can see it more clearly. Paint the top edge, where it meets the top cover, with a soft-edged brush so it blends into the cover in a more subtle way.

Adding the cover texture

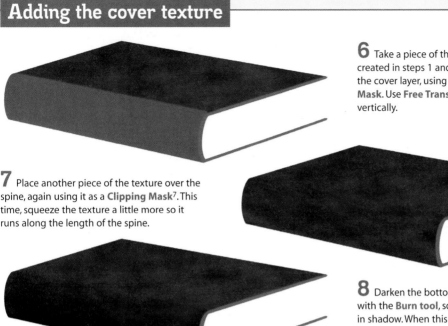

6 Take a piece of the leather texture we created in steps 1 and 2, and place this above the cover layer, using the cover as a **Clipping Mask**. Use **Free Transform** to compress it vertically.

7 Place another piece of the texture over the spine, again using it as a **Clipping Mask**[7]. This time, squeeze the texture a little more so it runs along the length of the spine.

8 Darken the bottom of the spine texture with the **Burn tool**, so that the bottom is more in shadow. When this is done, add a third piece of the texture over the right edge we drew in step 4.

The spine ridges

9 Draw a curved shape that follows the shape of the top of the spine, and fill with gray; add a little shading to the bottom half of it.

10 Place another piece of the leather texture over the top, using it as a **Clipping Mask**.

11 Duplicate the ridge layer and move it above the texture, adding an **Inner Bevel** using **Layer Styles.**

12 Change the mode of the copied layer to **Hard Light**, so we can see the texture through it.

13 Select an inner portion of the cover using the **Polygonal Lasso tool** or the **Pen tool**. Make a new **Curves Adjustment Layer**, and darken the selection, adding some red and blue for a different feel.

Duplicate the cover layer, and move the new layer to the bottom to make the back cover.

Drawing the paper

14 Start by drawing a paper shape on a new layer, between the covers and the back cover layer. Fill this with a pale tan.

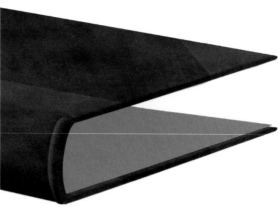

15 Load this layer as a selection, and nudge the selection up by one or two pixels. Then darken it, leaving a pale edge.

16 **Select All**, then Hold ⌥ *alt* as you nudge the sheet up with the cursor key. Release the ⌥ *alt* key and nudge up one more pixel with the cursor key.

17 Continue to build up all the sheets of paper in this way, sometimes nudging up by two pixels, sometimes three; nudge a few sheets left and right as well, to make a more random look.

18 When all the paper has been made, use **Filter > Blur > Gaussian Blur** with a value of just 0.5 pixels to smooth the paper out for a more natural appearance.

19 Ue the **Burn tool** to add shading beneath the cover and spine, so the paper looks more realistically lit.

Adding the title

GIBBON GIBBON GIBBON

THE
DECLINE
AND FALL
OF THE
ROMAN
EMPIRE

THE
DECLINE
AND FALL
OF THE
ROMAN
EMPIRE

THE
DECLINE
AND FALL
OF THE
ROMAN
EMPIRE

20 Set whatever title you like. Use a bold serif font, in keeping with the style of the book.

21 Use **Layer Styles** to create a shiny gold effect. With no background showing, select the title and choose **Copy Merged**.

22 Paste the merged copy, and use the **Image Warp** mode of **Free Transform** to apply a vertical **Arch** effect on the lettering.

23 Rotate the title and use **Free Transform** to stretch it vertically as required, so it fits neatly on the spine of the book.

Use the **Burn tool** to darken the bottom edge, in keeping with the shading on the spine.

The second book

24 The second book is a copy of the first, with a few amendments to make it differ. The covers are recolored to a redder tone than the original.

25 To make the front of the pages, duplicate the existing pages and flip the copy horizontally. Then use **Free Transform** to stretch the copy to the full width of the book.

26 Add some extra shading to the copied pages to darken them, imparting a different feel to the side pages.

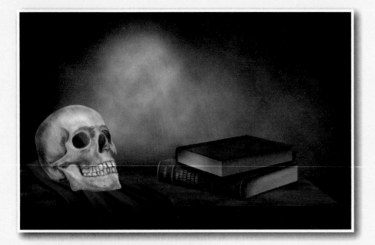

The candle

As the focus of attention, we need to make the candle both eyecatching and appealing. The dripping wax adds a natural, soft element, in contrast to the hard lines of the skull and the books; but it's the flickering flame that really catches the eye.

Overleaf, we'll draw the candle holder and then place the whole assembly on the page.

Shape and shading

1 Draw the candle shape in gray on a new layer. The sides must be parallel, with a gentle curve at the bottom to match the perspective of the scene. The top should look as if it has melted to some degree.

2 Paint a couple of drips on the side, then use the **Dodge and Burn tools** to add shading on the outside edges, as well as highlighting those two outer drips. Make the candle much darker right at the bottom, furthest from the light.

3 Use the **Dodge and Burn tools** to sketch in a couple of drips on the front of the candle: use the **Dodge tool** to paint the fronts, then the **Burn tool** to add shadows around the outside.

4 Lock the **Transparency** of the candle layer. Then use the **Smudge tool** to smear the shading into a more appealing shape. It's fairly easy to get a natural, flowing wax effect using this tool.

Color and highlights

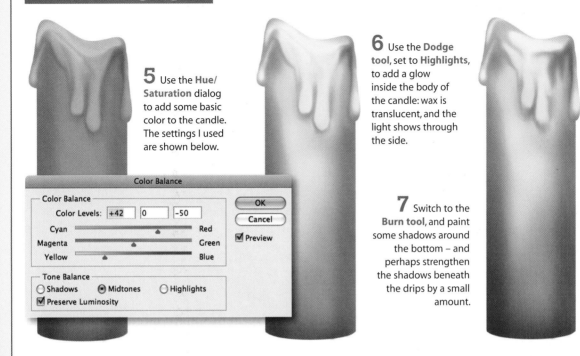

5 Use the **Hue/Saturation** dialog to add some basic color to the candle. The settings I used are shown below.

Color Balance

Color Balance
Color Levels: +42 0 -50

Cyan ——————▲———— Red
Magenta ———▲————————— Green
Yellow ——▲—————————— Blue

Tone Balance
○ Shadows ● Midtones ○ Highlights
☑ Preserve Luminosity

OK
Cancel
☑ Preview

6 Use the **Dodge tool**, set to **Highlights**, to add a glow inside the body of the candle: wax is translucent, and the light shows through the side.

7 Switch to the **Burn tool**, and paint some shadows around the bottom – and perhaps strengthen the shadows beneath the drips by a small amount.

Drawing the flame

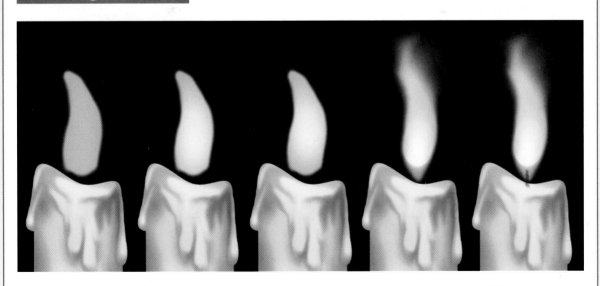

8 The flame is best seen on a dark background, so set the background to black. Draw the flame shape in orange on a new layer.

9 Use the **Dodge tool** to brighten the center of the flame, or paint inside it in white.

10 Choose a pale blue, and paint this at the bottom of the flame, just above the point where the wick would be.

11 Use the **Smudge tool** to create the flame shape. Use a large brush with a low opacity to smear the tip into a soft shape.

12 Finally, draw the wick on a new layer. Choose black, set the brush to **Dissolve** and draw a short line.

The candle holder

13 Draw the candle base in whatever shape you like. Start by drawing half the base, then flip a copy to make it symmetrical.

14 Use the **Burn tool** to add shading all around the edge of the candle holder.

15 Use the **Elliptical Marquee tool** to select a ring around the top, then **inverse** the selection and darken beneath it.

16 Continue to make elliptical selections, adding shading above and below as needed to bring out the forms of the candle holder.

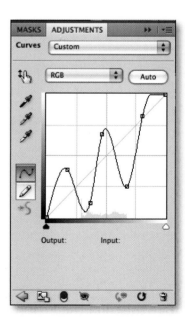

17 Use the **Burn tool** again to darken the lower surfaces – beneath the upper rim, beneath the midpoint ring, and around the base of the whole holder.

18 Make a new **Curves Adjustment Layer**, using the candle holder as a **Clipping Mask**. Drag the curve into an up/down shape as seen here – see page 16 for more details.

Looking through Curves

19 We can see the effect of the Curves operation on the left. As we can see, it's not quite perfect.

20 While we 'look through' the **Curves** adjustment, we can continue to work on the candle holder with **Dodge and Burn**. But be prepared for unpredictable results, due to the adjustment!

21 Make an elliptical selection around the base of the holder, and use the **Burn tool** to darken it, adding another layer of detail.

22 Load up the candle holder as a selection, and make a new **Hard Light** layer using it as a **Clipping Mask**. Use the **Burn tool** to paint a dark rim directly beneath the candle.

Final shading

23 When we place the whole candle assembly on the page, it looks too bright: so darken the **Hard Light** layer we created in step 22, to make the whole holder a little more dull.

24 If we add some color to the **Hard Light** layer, it will have its effect on the holder beneath. Add a little red and yellow using **Color Balance**[10] to give the holder a warmer tint.

25 When we now use the **Dodge and Burn** tools on the **Hard Light** layer, set to **Highlights**, they affect the color as well as the brightness: this exaggerates the tones, allowing us to bring in the effect of reflected candle light.

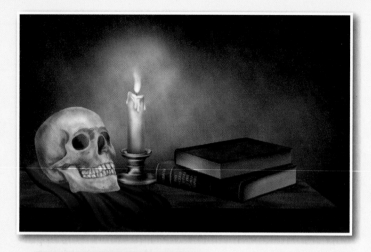

The metronome

The metronome adds an indication of passing time to the illustration, neatly counterpointing the skull as an image of mortality.

Starting with a simple wooden box, the only tricky part is drawing the scale that indicates the tempo: the spacing of the ticks is an awkward scale, and each number needs to be positioned individually for it to represent the scale correctly.

Shape and texture

1 Draw the outline of the metronome on a new layer, using the **Pen tool** to allow repositioning of the vertices.

2 To soften the corners, use the **Refine Edge** technique as described on page 179.

3 Place a copy of the wood texture on top, set to **Multiply** mode; darken the faces as needed.

4 Draw a black shape within the metronome to mark out the interior of the device.

5 Select an inner edge on the right and top of the interior, and make a new layer from it. Add another piece of the wood texture to it, and darken to make the edge look real.

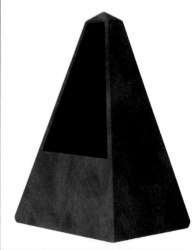
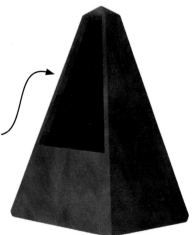

Finishing the case

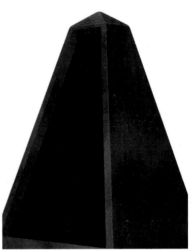

6 The feet are made from circular selections of the wood texture, shaded with the **Burn tool** to make them appear rounded.

7 Scratches can be added using the technique described on page 80 – paint on a layer to which an **Inner Bevel** has been applied to draw fine lines.

8 On a new layer, draw over all the edges with a hard-edged white **Brush**, then lower the transparency of the layer to just 10%.

The tempo scale

9 Start with a narrow gray rectangle, on a new layer.

10 Type the numbers very small, with even leading. These are the numbers used on most metronomes: 40, 44, 48, 52, 56, 60, 66, 72, 80, 88, 96, 104, 112, 120, 132, 144, 160, 176, 190, 208.

11 Duplicate the numbers and increase them to fall between the existing numbers. Draw tick lines beneath each number, both on the right and on the left.

12 Spacing out the numbers and ticks takes a little time. Select all but the top row, and nudge down 12 pixels. Then select all but the top two rows, and nudge down 18 pixels. Continue in this way, nudging each new line 6 pixels more than the previous pair.

13 Select the right hand row of numbers, and move them down so they're spaced roughly equidistant between the numbers on the right.

14 Finally, add vertical lines and the standard music terms at the appropriate places. Add a small **Inner Bevel** to the layer to make the numbers appear recessed.

Placing the scale in position

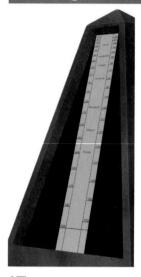

15 Use **Free Transform** to distort the scale so it fits within the cavity in the metronome.

16 Use **Dodge and Burn** to add diagonal streaks of light and shade, as the start of the metallic process.

17 Add a metallic **Curves** adjustment to complete the metal, as seen on page 16.

18 The ticker bar is made from a piece of the original scale, shaded and with the same **Curves** adjustment.

The weight

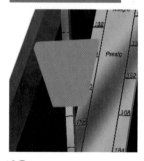

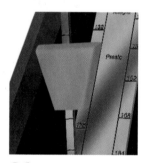

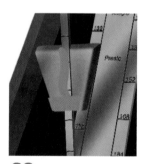

19 Draw the weight on a new layer, and fill with gray.

20 Select the top and right edges, feather the selection and darken them a little.

21 Apply the same **Curves** adjustment to make the weight appear more metallic.

22 Draw the clip on a new layer, filled with gray.

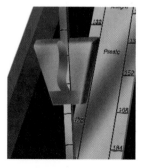

23 Use **Dodge and Burn** again to add shading to the weight, giving it a dull metal feel.

24 Make two small circular selections, and use **Dodge and Burn** to make them appear rounded. Then select and darken the back edge, and draw straight lines through them to give the impression of tiny screw heads.

The key

25 The keyhole is an elliptical selection with a metal **Inner Bevel** effect (see page 18). The hole is a black ellipse.

26 Draw the key on a new layer. As always, draw half and then flip a copy to make the other half.

27 Use **Dodge and Burn** to add shading to the key.

28 Select the key, and nudge a copy down and to the right; inverse and darken the outside.

29 Use the **Curves** adjustment to make the key appear metallic, and paint the end black as it goes into the hole.

Finishing off

30 Duplicate the ticker assembly, merge the layers and fill with black; soften to make the shadow.

31 Draw the top restraining latch on a new layer, inside the reveal of the metronome.

32 Use **Dodge and Burn** and the same **Curves** adjustment to make it metallic.

33 Finally, I've added a new **Curves Adjustment Layer** above the wood to darken the whole metronome, giving it a richer, mahogany appearance.

The glass

Glass objects can be among the hardest items to draw in Photoshop. The trick lies in distorting the refracted view seen through them: while a glass may never look perfect on a white background, once it has an image to work with the whole thing comes to life.

The basic glass

1 Start by drawing half an outline of a glass, in gray, on a new layer. Flip a copy horizontally to make the other half. Make the base as an ellipse on a separate layer.

2 Use the **Burn tool** to add some basic shading, keeping just within the outline of the glass.

3 Use the **Dodge and Burn tools** to add more shading to the glass, down the stem and creating a highlight on the edge.

4 Lock the **Transparency** of the glass layer, and use the **Smudge tool** to smear the highlights and shadows into a more natural form.

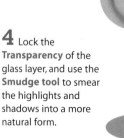

The stem

5 Add some shading to the base, using **Dodge and Burn** once more.

6 Load up the base as a selection, and nudge the selection up a couple of pixels; then **inverse** the selection and shade the edge.

7 Repeat this process in reverse for the upper edge, and use the **Smudge** tool to smear the highlights into a more swirling shape.

The glass in the illustration

8 Merge the glass layers together, and place it in the image. Make a selection around it, and hide it; make a **Merged Copy** of the background, and **Paste**, using the glass as a **Clipping Mask**. Use **Filter > Liquify** to distort the pasted background, as seen through the glass, then add a **Layer Mask** and paint out the left, highlighted side.

9 Place a copy of the original glass on top, and set its layer mode to **Hard Light**. When we now see the background through it, the glass is more impressive.

10 Select a wine region within the glass, and fill with red on a new layer. Set the new layer's mode to **Multiply**, so we can still see the glass through it.

11 Duplicate the glass layer again, and place above the wine layer, using that layer as a **Clipping Mask**[7]. Now, the shine shows up over the wine properly.

12 Add a new **Hard Light** layer above the glass, using it as a **Clipping Mask**, and paint shadows on the side away from the light source.

Finishing off: adding shadows

1 Here's the intial view of the skull, red cloth and table. Although they're all sitting together, we need to add a serious amount of shading to make the assembly look convincing.

2 Make a new layer above the table, using the table as a **Clipping Mask**. Paint on here in black using a large soft-edged **Brush**, adding shadows beneath the cloth and away from the direction of the light source.

3 To make the skull look more as if it's on the fabric, we can add a **Layer Mask** and paint out the bottom edge, as if a fold in the cloth has fallen in front of it. This goes a long way toward unifying the two elements: making them interact with each other makes them look more like they're both part of the same scene.

4 Add a shadow layer above the cloth, and paint shadows beneath the skull. I've also added a **Curves Adjustment Layer** above the skull to darken it up slightly, so it's less bright in the final composition.

Make a new layer, using the skull as a **Clipping Mask**, and paint deep shadows away from the light source.

Making the reflection

5 Duplicate the book, candle holder and glass layers. We don't need to flip the book vertically: simply slide it down, beneath the book, and flip just the shading and the title. Similarly, the base of the glass can just be slid down behind the original; only the stem needs to be flipped vertically.

6 Place all the reflected layers into a new **Layer Group**, so we can work on the group as a whole. Change the opacity to around 40%, and set the mode of the group to **Hard Light**; this creates a realistic-looking reflection.

Final touches

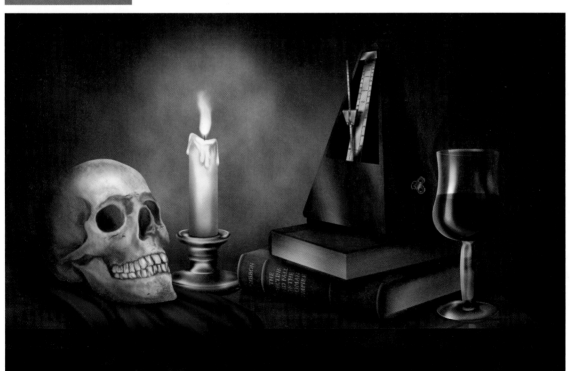

7 To finish off, make a selection the shape of the metronome and the books, feather the edges and fill with black to make the shadow of those objects cast on the wall. Add new layers beneath, between and above the books, and paint shadows with a soft-edged **Brush**. Finally, rotate a copy of the wine glass above the metronome and reduce its opacity to make its reflection.

Index

brush

200, 201, 206, 218, 219

About the author

AUTHOR PHOTOGRAPH BY KATE GARNER

Steve Caplin is a freelance digital artist and author working in London, England. His satirical photomontage work is regularly commissioned by newspapers and magazines both in the United Kingdom and around the world.

Steve's work for advertising agencies has won two Campaign Poster Awards and a D&AD award. He has lectured widely in England, Norway, France and Holland, and has taught digital design at the University of Westminster and the University of the Arts London.

He is the author of several books, including *How to Cheat in Photoshop* (six editions), *How to Cheat in Photoshop Elements* (co-authored), *Icon Design*, *Max Pixel's Adventures in Adobe Photoshop Elements*, and *The Complete Guide to Digital Illustration* (co-authored). He has also co-authored four mainstream books: *Dad Stuff* (published in the United States as *Be the Coolest Dad on the Block*), *More Dad Stuff*, *Stuff the Turkey* and *Complete and Utter Zebu*.

Steve runs **www.thefullmontage.com**, a resource library for photomontage artists. It provides picture elements of all kinds, from complex cutouts to transparency, and includes the innovative ReadyMade drag and drop objects.

A regular contributor to *MacUser* magazine since 1990, Steve is also a beta tester for Adobe Photoshop and thinks the iPhone is the best thing he has ever owned.

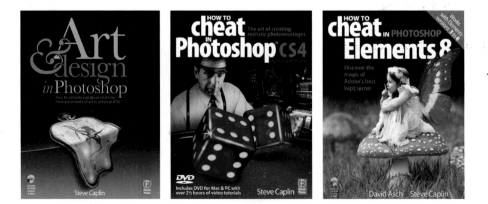